Software Architecture Foundation - 2nd Edition

Other publications by Van Haren Publishing

Van Haren Publishing (VHP) specializes in titles on Best Practices, methods and standards within four domains:
- IT and IT Management
- Architecture (Enterprise and IT)
- Business Management and
- Project Management

Van Haren Publishing is also publishing on behalf of leading organizations and companies: BRMI, CA, Centre Henri Tudor, CATS CM, Gaming Works, IACCM, IAOP, IFDC, Innovation Value Institute, IPMA-NL, ITSqc, NAF, KNVI, PMI-NL, PON, The Open Group, The SOX Institute.

Topics are (per domain):

IT and IT Management	Enterprise Architecture	Business Management
ABC of ICT	ArchiMate®	*BABOK® Guide*
ASL®	GEA®	BiSL® and BiSL® Next
CMMI®	Novius Architectuur	BRMBOK™
COBIT®	Methode	BTF
e-CF	TOGAF®	CATS CM®
ISM		DID®
ISO/IEC 20000	**Project Management**	EFQM
ISO/IEC 27001/27002	A4-Projectmanagement	eSCM
ISPL	DSDM/Atern	IACCM
IT4IT®	ICB / NCB	ISA-95
IT-CMF™	ISO 21500	ISO 9000/9001
IT Service CMM	MINCE®	OPBOK
ITIL®	M_o_R®	SixSigma
MOF	MSP®	SOX
MSF	P3O®	SqEME®
SABSA	*PMBOK® Guide*	
SAF	Praxis®	
SIAM™	PRINCE2®	
TRIM		
VeriSM™		
XLA®		

For the latest information on VHP publications, visit our website: www.vanharen.net.

Software Architecture Foundation

CPSA-F® Exam Preparation

Gernot Starke, Alexander Lorz

Colophon

Title	Software Architecture Foundation
	CPSA-F® Exam Preparation
Authors:	Gernot Starke, Alexander Lorz
Publisher:	Van Haren Publishing, 's-Hertogenbosch-NL
	www.vanharen.net.
ISBN Hard copy:	978 94 018 1042 5
ISBN eBook (pdf):	978 94 018 1043 2
ISBN ePUB:	978 94 018 1044 9
Edition:	Second edition, first impression, June 2023
Layout and Design:	Coco Bookmedia, Amersfoort-NL
Copyright:	© Van Haren Publishing, 2021, 2023

Contents

Quick overview

This book covers everything you need to master the iSAQB® Certified Professional for Software Architecture - Foundation Level (CPSA-F®) certification.

This internationally renowned education and certification schema defines various learning paths for practical software architects.

This book concentrates on the Foundation Level examination. It explains and clarifies all 40+ learning goals in the current 2023 version of the CPSA-F® curriculum. In addition, you will find a step-by-step preparation guide for the examination.

Please beware: This book is *not* meant as a replacement for existing software architecture books and courses, but strongly focuses on explaining and clarifying the iSAQB CPSA-F foundation.

Foreword by Mirko Hillert

As a sub-discipline of software engineering, software architecture acquired an increasing importance in the 1990s, both in industrial and academic environments. This IT discipline has developed rapidly since then, and nowadays there is consensus among experts that it is the architecture of a software system that decisively determines its quality. In the course of this steadily increasing importance of software architectures, the specific occupational profile of software architects within development teams evolved. This complex role can hardly be mastered today without profound knowledge of common technologies and frameworks as well as methodical and communicative skills.

Ever since its foundation as a non-profit organization in 2008, the International Software Architecture Qualification Board (iSAQB®) has been working steadily to establish an internationally recognized standard in education and training of software architects. And with great success: Over 24,000 IT professionals worldwide have already been certified within the scope of the Certified Professional for Software Architecture (CPSA®) certification scheme developed by the iSAQB.

The new book by Dr. Alexander Lorz and Dr. Gernot Starke offers a comprehensive compendium of basic knowledge in modern software architecture to anyone who wants to embark on the career path of a software architect. In excellent didactic and content-related manner, it conveys all the necessary fields of knowledge that are required in order to pass the Certified Professional for Software Architecture (CPSA®) exam at Foundation Level. It is equally suitable for self-study as well as accompanying literature for CPSA-Foundation Level training courses.

Both authors are long-standing members of the iSAQB Foundation Level working group and have played a leading role in shaping the content of the curriculum and the examination, based upon their many years of experience in both practical software engineering and teaching technical subjects to a wide variety of audiences.

I wish you, the reader, many new insights from this book, and much success on your way as a software architect.

Mirko Hillert
CEO of iSAQB GmbH, Berlin.
Responsible for iSAQB international activities.

Foreword by Stefan Tilkov

Software architecture belongs to the main success factors in modern software development. It enables the development of high-quality software systems and the flexible adaption of these to changing requirements, and technologies. In addition, software architecture facilitates delivering on schedule, and helps teams to work cost-efficiently, for the entire life span of systems.

For more than a decade, the international Software Architecture Qualification Board (iSAQB) has succeeded in establishing a diverse set of widely accepted curricula and learning paths for this important engineering discipline, for both foundational and advanced topics. During this time, Gernot and Alexander have helped to shape the Foundation Level curriculum and exams into their current form.

In this book, they share their understanding of methodological and practical software architecture and software engineering with a focus on the preparation for the iSAQB CPSA-F exam. They combine their didactical and practical experience from numerous training sessions and industry projects to provide a concise and profound introduction into the relevant topics of Foundation Level training.

Over the years I have taught numerous software architecture classes myself.

A book like this, covering all the different learning goals, is a very welcome companion and study guide for learners.

It will complement your training sessions and I am sure it will help you towards a better understanding of software architecture and a successful CPSA Foundation Level exam.

Stefan Tilkov
CEO INNOQ Deutschland GmbH, vice president of iSAQB e.V.
Twitter: @stilkov

Foreword by Peter Hruschka

I began teaching design classes in the late 70s, when software architects were still called chief programmers, chief designers or lead designers. Since then the body of knowledge about software and system architecture has increased dramatically. But even in 2021 I feel that the role of software architects is the least understood role in IT. Every other role has a clearer definition: project manager, requirements engineer, programmer, tester...

Helping to improve this situation was a key reason for me to join the iSAQB right from the beginning. The iSAQB has achieved a lot in the last decade, increasing the awareness of the importance of that role and providing curricula as a basis for education and training.

This book by Gernot and Alex is a further important milestone to spread the news about this fascinating but challenging role.

It will help future software architects to better understand the Foundation Level curriculum and prepare themselves for the iSAQB CPSA-F exam.

Hopefully, it will also trigger many new companies in various countries of the world to create training courses based on this book, thus increasing the number of highly educated software architects.

I am looking forward to better designed, trustworthy and enjoyable software intensive products and systems.

Dr. Peter Hruschka
Atlantic Systems Guild,
Co-founder and member of both iSAQB and IREB, consultant and author.

Part I: Introduction

This part explains what this book is all about and introduces you to the iSAQB e.V.[1] standardization organization and their Software Architecture Certification, especially the *Certified Professional for Software Architecture - Foundation Level* (CPSA-F)[2].

This internationally renowned education and certification schema defines both the subject and corresponding examinations.

Content overview

In this first part, we will answer several fundamental questions:

- Why software architecture?
- Why we wrote this book?
- What is the *International Software Architecture Qualification Board*, iSAQB?
- What benefits are to be gained from a CPSA-F certification?

Next, we:

- Introduce the iSAQB Foundation curriculum.
- Explain the iSAQB Foundation examination process.
- Show various ways to prepare for the iSAQB Foundation examination.

About Software Architecture

What is the typical life span of the IT systems you work on? If you ponder this question for a while, you may come up with a surprisingly long period of time. Many systems we encountered have existed for years and may continue to do so for even longer. Often, they originated as a small system and evolved into a product or other long-term venture.

During such a long time, a lot of things are subject to change: Functionalities and features adapt to shifting customer requirements and business goals. Technologies which the architecture relied upon are no longer available. Experienced people leave the development team, whilst project and product management changes.

Most software systems have to continuously adapt to such changes in requirements, technologies and even team and organizational structures. The *field of software architecture* is the engineering science that enables this adaptation process in an environment which is constrained by factors like cost, time

---

1 https://isaqb.org
2 iSAQB (the International Software Architecture Qualification Board) has copyrighted and trademarked its curricula, logos and other intellectual property. In this book we will not append the ® symbol at every possible occasion. All rights remain with the iSAQB e.V.

to market and availability of sufficiently skilled humans. The *software architecture of an IT system* is decisive for feasibility, cost- and time-efficiency of its future development: Better architectures lead to better time-to-market and lower maintenance and operational cost.

> *"The goal of software architecture is to minimize the human resources required to build and maintain the required system."*

Robert C. Martin

Besides technical decisions, software architecture deals with efficient use of *human resources*, therefore minimizing development and operational costs. It goes way beyond finding a great technical solution, as it aims to find compromises between the sometimes conflicting goals of all stakeholders.

Software architecture helps to achieve qualities like maintainability, reliability, safety, performance, security, scalability and operability. It reduces complexity by breaking systems down into manageable units with defined dependencies, therefore enabling efficient communication and reasoning about the inner workings of systems. Software architecture defines rules and technical decisions to guide the development, maintenance and operation of systems.

About this book

There are already a number of well-established books on software architecture (see Appendix C References for a curated and opinionated list), so why did we write another one?

In contrast to existing books, this one completely covers the iSAQB curriculum in a sufficiently detailed yet compact way and can serve as an efficient and effective study guide.

You will find numerous sample questions, helping you to prepare for the CPSA-F examination.

In case you're interested in our (Alexander's and Gernot's) motivation to write this book - we included some information about ourselves in Appendix A.

Conventions used in this book

 Relevant for the examination: Boxes like this one contain tips or hints that are especially relevant for the iSAQB examination.

 General tips for your architecture: Boxes like this one contain tips or hints that can help to improve your software architecture work in general, which might be relevant for the iSAQB examination.

ℹ️ Special information: Sometimes we want to focus your attention - that's where we use information boxes like this.

Our assumptions about you

When writing this book, we had several (potentially silly) assumptions about you (the readers) in mind:

- You work in IT (information technology) and have loads of work to do. Therefore, you want this book to be (relatively) short and compact.
- You have prior experience in developing software systems, and at least a basic understanding of computer programming.
- You want to forward your professional career by passing the iSAQB CPSA-Foundation examination. You may not yet be familiar with some of the iSAQB specific terms, so we have included a glossary, see Appendix B.
- You already have access to books or other resources on software engineering, so we won't repeat all the basics in this book.
- Some of you might want to teach the iSAQB curriculum to others. You rightfully expect a detailed explanation of what is meant by all the learning objectives included in the iSAQB curriculum. In that case, you may be interested in references to additional textbooks and other sources, so you can prepare your personal training material.

Structure of this book

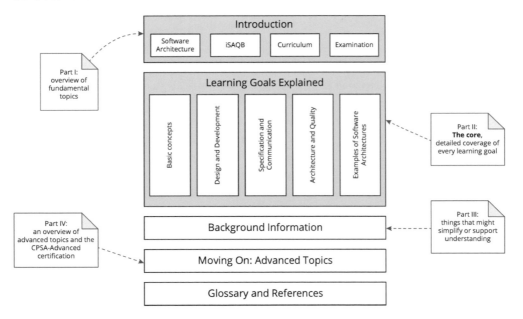

About iSAQB

 The *International Software Architecture Qualification Board* is a non-profit organization with members from industry, development and consulting firms, education, academia and other organizations.

It is established as an *association* (e.V.) according to German law with the following objectives:
- Creating and maintaining a consistent *curriculum* for software architects.
- Defining certification examinations based upon the various CPSA curricula.
- Ensuring high quality of teaching and further training for software architects.
- Ensuring a high quality of certification.

iSAQB defines and prescribes training and examination regulations, but does not carry out any training or examinations itself. iSAQB trainings are delivered by licensed training providers while examinations are handled by separate certifying bodies.

iSAQB monitors and audits the quality of these trainings and all associated processes (e.g. certification and examination procedures).

iSAQB closes a gap

Software architecture is a relatively young discipline, which is diversely discussed in the IT community despite many publications. There are many different perceptions regarding the roles and responsibilities of software architects and many development projects establish their own understanding.

In other IT disciplines such as project management, business analysis and requirements engineering, or testing, a wider and more generally accepted consensus on job descriptions exists. A variety of independent organizations are offering curricula, that clearly state what knowledge and skills should be transferred in trainings to the participants: e.g., for requirements engineering the IREB[3] (International Requirements Engineering Board) sets world-wide standards, for project management there are several organizations with a slightly different focus, like PMI[4], and for testers the ISTQB[5] (International Software Testing Qualification Board) sets the standards. For software architecture, this gap is bridged by the iSAQB.

---

3   https://www.ireb.org/
4   https://www.pmi.org/
5   https://www.istqb.org/

Levels of iSAQB education and certification

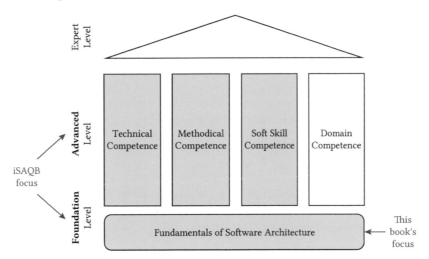

Figure 0.1 Levels of iSAQB Education and Certification

How iSAQB works

Please refer to the iSAQB website for detailed information on how the iSAQB association works, how to apply for membership, etc. For the sake of this book, it is sufficient to note that membership is open to anyone interested in software architecture, and that the heterogeneous structure of iSAQB members allows for well-balanced professional discussions.

The publicly available curricula provide full transparency on all learning goals.

The various curricula are maintained by distinct working groups and curators. For the Foundation Level, the following stakeholders are of particular importance:

Foundation Level Working Group (FLWG)

An iSAQB working group, consisting of volunteer software architecture experts from various domains. This group maintains both the curriculum and the corresponding examination questions to ensure strict compliance between those two artifacts. The curriculum is maintained in an open manner on GitHub https://github.com/isaqb-org/. Everybody is free to propose changes and report errors or omissions. The FLWG will publish a new and updated version of the curriculum once every two years, balancing the need for regular updates, and the need for stability in trainings and examinations.

On the other hand, examination questions are strictly confidential, and therefore are managed privately within this working group.

All decisions regarding the content of the CPSA-Foundation Level curriculum are handled by this working group. Major changes have to be approved by the iSAQB executive board.

Certification bodies

Commercial enterprises that organize and conduct the actual examinations. iSAQB ensures the strict independence of education and examination. No certification body is allowed to conduct training, and no training provider is allowed to conduct or organize examinations.

Audit Group

An iSAQB working group that actively monitors the quality of education and examination through inspections and reviews. Trainers, training providers and certification bodies are all subject to such audits.

Open and transparent

Although the content of the iSAQB curriculum is copyrighted, all work related to the curriculum is carried out in *open source* manner:

- The curricula are maintained in public repositories on GitHub, https://github.com/isaqb-org.
- Comments and change requests are maintained as GitHub-issues.
- Current versions of the curriculum are available on https://isaqb-org.github.io/.

The iSAQB distinguishes between numerous topics, with the Foundation Level being just one of these. Every topic in the advanced level has its own curriculum, see section *iSAQB examination overview*, for details.

About certification

Before we dive into the details of certification and examination, let's clarify the terminology:

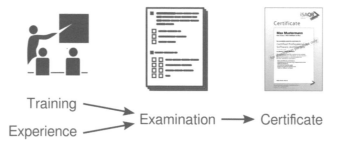

- First of all, you should expand your knowledge of the subject area: Enhance your own professional experience with training, reading, and other means of education. This will provide you with the required knowledge and skills.
- In the examination you have to demonstrate your capabilities and level of comprehension regarding software architecture. Your examination will be scored, and you will pass the exam if you achieve at least 60% of the maximum possible score.
- After successfully passing the examination, you will receive a certificate.

Why certification?

With the iSAQB certification you gain some compelling advantages. In particular it:

1. Helps you gain competitive advantage and can positively differentiate you from other professionals;
2. Significantly increases your financial earning potential;
3. Improves your professional credibility;
4. Connects you with the growing community of software architecture experts;
5. Demonstrates your commitment to continuous learning and improvement;
6. Provides a methodical foundation for day-to-day architecture decisions;
7. Exposes you to methodical approaches beyond your daily development and project work;
8. Proves that you have dealt intensively with relevant topics around software architectures.

As the iSAQB is strictly vendor-independent and technology-neutral, their certifications are not limited to certain domains.

On the other hand: Successful certification does not automatically enable you to develop and deploy better software architectures. But a university degree in computer science does not guarantee that either. Nevertheless, most students try to achieve a formal completion of their efforts, as organizations and enterprises commonly pay attention to such formalities.

iSAQB certifications have lifetime validity

In alignment with higher educational degrees (like bachelor, master, PhD and others), iSAQB certifications *are valid forever* and do not need to be renewed.

Other certification bodies require graduates to regularly renew and to regularly pay additional fees for this renewal. This is not the case here

iSAQB Foundation

The title of this section (iSAQB Foundation) is a shortened version of the *official* name "iSAQB Certified Professional for Software Architecture - Foundation Level". As that 8-word monster is a little difficult to pronounce, we've cut it down to "iSAQB Foundation". This section provides a brief overview of the curriculum for this certification level and helps you to plan your personal preparation for the examination.

iSAQB Foundation Level curriculum

The Foundation Level curriculum [iSAQB-FLC] consists of the following chapters:

1. Basic concepts of software architecture: Roles and tasks of software architects, important results, cooperation with other stakeholders.
2. Design and development of software architectures:
   - How can you design structures and concepts systematically? This is the most important part of the CPSA-F curriculum and also the part that has the greatest significance for the practical work of software architects.

- Design principles and the most important architecture and design patterns.
3. Specification and communication of software architectures:
   - How and what should you document?
   - How do you communicate your ideas, concepts, and decisions with other stakeholders?
4. Software architecture and quality:
   - How can you systematically achieve the required qualities of your system?
   - How can you analyze, evaluate and diagnose your design?
5. Examples of software architectures: Software architects should be aware of good and bad examples of architectures and should discuss solutions with peers - beyond the horizon of their own experience.

What do you learn in the CPSA-Foundation Level training?

Graduates of the iSAQB CPSA-Foundation Level examination will have the knowledge and skills required for designing and documenting a specific software architecture based on a sufficiently detailed requirements specification for small and medium-sized systems. They will be equipped with the methodical tools and abilities to enable them to make problem-specific design decisions on the basis of their previously acquired practical experience.

What is NOT covered in the CPSA-F training?

The iSAQB Foundation Level curriculum reflects the contents currently considered by iSAQB members to be necessary and useful for achieving the CPSA-F learning goals.

It is not a comprehensive description of the entire domain of *software architecture*.

The following topics or concepts are *not* part of the CPSA-F curriculum:
- Concrete implementation technologies, frameworks or libraries;
- Programming or programming languages;
- Fundamentals or notations of modeling languages (such as UML, SysML, BPMN or BPEL);
- System analysis and requirements engineering (please refer to the education and certification program of IREB, the International Requirements Engineering Board);
- Software testing (please refer to the education and certification program of ISTQB, the International Software Testing Board);
- Project or product management;
- Specific software or development tools.

iSAQB examination overview

Prerequisites for CPSA-F certification

Candidates aiming to achieve the iSAQB CPSA-Foundation certification require prior knowledge and experience. In particular, substantial practical experience of software development in a team environment is required for understanding the learning materials and considerably increases your prospects of successfully passing the examination.

We consider the following prerequisites to be essential:

- More than 18 months of practical experience with software development, gained through team-based development of several systems outside of formal education.
- Knowledge of, and practical experience with, at least one higher programming language, especially:
  - concepts of modularization (packages, namespaces etc.), parameter passing (call-by value, call-by-reference) and scope (type and variable declaration and definition);
  - basics of type systems (static vs. dynamic typing, generic data types);
  - error and exception handling in software;
  - potential problems of global state and global variables.
- Basics knowledge of:
  - modeling and abstraction;
  - algorithms and data structures (i.e. Lists, Trees, Hash tables, Dictionary, Map);
  - UML (class, package, component and sequence diagrams) and their relation to source code;
  - approaches to testing of software (e.g. unit- and acceptance testing).

Furthermore, the following will be useful for understanding several concepts:

- Basics and differences of imperative, declarative, object-oriented and functional programming.
- Practical experience in:
  - a higher level programming language;
  - designing and implementing distributed applications, such as client-server systems or web applications;
  - technical documentation, especially documenting source code, system design or technical concepts.

> In CPSA-Foundation examinations, there might be questions covering these prerequisites. None of these questions concern specific programming languages or programming constructs.

Relevance of topics for the examination

The curriculum contains prioritized learning goals. For each learning goal, the relevance for the examination of this learning goal or its sub-elements is explicitly stated through the use of a relevance classification as described in the table below.

Relevance class	Learning goal category	Interpretation
R1	Being able to. . .	Will be part of the examination. These are the contents that graduates are expected to be able to apply themselves.
R2	Understanding. . .	May be part of the examination. Graduates are expected to understand these contents in principle, but not necessarily to apply them themselves.
R3	Knowing. . .	This will not be part of the examination. Graduates should know about the topic.

Examination process

The examination is a written multiple-choice test, which can currently be taken *paper-based* or as an electronic assessment, either online or in a test center. That choice depends on the certification body[6] you choose.

You can find an overview, including contact information, on the iSAQB website https://isaqb.org.

The iSAQB e.V. strictly enforces a clear organizational separation of education (training, coaching) and the examination itself:
- Trainers and coaches are never allowed to conduct examinations.
- Certification bodies are never allowed to conduct trainings or perform coaching.

All examinations consist of approximately 40-45 multiple choice questions.

The complete examination has a maximum duration of 75 minutes, which can be prolonged by 15 minutes for those candidates where the language used in the examination is not their native language, though this requires a prior request. For example, if you are a native Spanish speaker and the exam is conducted in English, you will be granted an additional 15 minutes.

Earlier submission is possible.

Each question will earn you from 1 to 3 points, depending on the level of difficulty and the length of the question.

The maximum achievable score is always shown in the question header. As a general principle, the points for correct answers are totaled up and candidates need at least 60% of the achievable maximum score to pass the examination.

---

6   As of March 2023 the iSAQB cooperates with about a dozen licensed certification bodies.

Some additional facts to keep in mind:

- No aids, tools, books or notes of any kind are allowed in the examination.
- Remote proctored online examinations may require you to scan your surroundings with your webcam and you might not be allowed to have additional monitors in your field of view. Some exam providers also prohibit the use of head-sets.
- You may leave the room[7] as soon as you're finished, but you are not allowed to return. You may stay until the time is over.
- You are required to present an official identification document (passport etc.) with a photo of yourself prior to the examination.
- Taking notes on additional sheets of paper besides the official exam paper is allowed, but that paper must be submitted together with the examination.
- Examinees will be notified of their examination result in writing by the certification body. The printed certificate will be shipped by the certification body to the address given by the participant at the beginning of the examination form, unless a certification body decides to issue digitally signed documents instead.
- Double-check the information in the header of the examination form to ensure that your name will be spelled correctly on the certificate.
- If applicable, make sure that the certifier knows in advance that you are a non-native speaker in order to get extra time.

❗ Examination material is strictly confidential.
⬤ Every participant of iSAQB examinations is personally required to sign a confidentiality agreement. They may not disclose, make public or otherwise pass on any examination questions or corresponding answers.

Types of examination questions
The iSAQB uses three different types of examination questions, all of which are described below.

❗ Visual layout will be different in original examination.
⬤ The visual layout of the original questions will most likely differ from the layout shown here, but the types of questions are exactly identical!

Single choice questions (marked with "A" for Assortment)
You shall select one answer from a list of possibilities.
Only one answer is correct.
Depending on the question, you have to mark the only correct or the only wrong option. Example of an A-question:

---

7   Online exams are conducted in a supervised manner. In this case there is also an upper limit for the time available, but no lower limit.

A-question: Which of the following is an animal: (1 point)

[ ] Carrot

[x] Cat

[ ] Computer

[ ] Chaos

Pick from many (marked with "P")

You shall select two or more from a (larger) number of options. The expected number of answers will always be clearly stated. Example of a P-question:

P-question: From the following list of tools, select the two (2) most important tools for software development: (1 point)

[x] Compiler

[x] Editor

[ ] Hammer

[ ] Nail

[ ] Coffee machine

Remarks:

- Every correct answer yields a fraction of the available points (in our example, 0.5 points).
- For every wrong answer, the same fraction is subtracted from this question's score. In the example, one correct and one wrong answer yields zero points in total.
- Leaving out a correct option is neutral: Marking fewer options than expected will NOT lead to any subtraction of points. In the example, if you only select one (correct) option, you get a score of 0.5 points.
- In P-questions, more options than you are supposed to select might seem to be applicable. Here you're expected, based upon your experience and knowledge, to judge which options are better suited than others. A coffee machine is certainly useful for software developers, but other items from this list are more important.

Allocation questions (marked with "K" from German "Klärungsfrage"[8])

For each option given you are supposed to decide between one of two choices, e.g. between "right/wrong", "applicable/non applicable", "static/dynamic". For every option given, there will always be exactly one correct choice. Example of a K-question:

---

8   Yes, we know. This is weird.

K-question: For every animal given below, choose if it lives in water or on land: (1 point)

water	land	
[x]	[ ]	Dolphin
[ ]	[x]	Horse
[ ]	[x]	Cat
[x]	[ ]	Octopus

Remarks:

- Every correct answer gives a fraction of the available points (in our example, 0.25 point).
- For every wrong answer, a fraction is subtracted from this question's score. In the example, two correct and two wrong answers yields zero points in sum.
- Leaving out an answer is neutral (zero points). In the example, giving only three (correct) answers yields 0.75 point.

Important note for all types of questions

- The type of questions and the number of answers to be selected are always clearly indicated in the examination form or in the corresponding online system.
- Pay attention to the maximum number of options to be selected. Giving more answers than asked for always results in 0 points for the corresponding question.
- Giving fewer answers than asked for is not punished. In case of doubt, you are better leaving out an answer to avoid getting points subtracted for picking a wrong answer. Please consider this advice seriously and do not take unnecessary risks. A bird in the hand is worth two in the bush.
- The minimum score you can receive for a single question is 0 points. Even if you have ticked more wrong options than correct ones, the penalty applied will not propagate beyond the scope of a question. So guessing is still an option exactly when (and only when) you don't know any of the answers at all.

Preparation for the Foundation Level examination

You can prepare yourself for the iSAQB CPSA-F examination by attending licensed trainings, or by self-study. In this section you will find some hints for both approaches. At first sight, these recommendations might appear similar, but they differ hugely in terms of the amount of time that should be invested for preparation.

Preparation by attending a training course

The most efficient way to prepare for the iSAQB examination is to participate in a three or four day training course, given by an accredited training provider.

The more experience your trainer has, the more benefit you will gain from such training.

Nevertheless, you should seek to enhance your training by undertaking the following steps, allowing approximately 2-4 hours for this:

1. (10 minutes) Skim through the list of learning goals (see introduction of Part II). If you encounter any terms you don't know, ask your trainer for an explanation.
2. (1-2 hours) Read all the learning goals in Part II of this book. Concentrate on the R1 relevance (as those will most likely be part of your examination). Mark all keywords or concepts you're unfamiliar with:
   - Look up those keywords in the glossary;
   - Briefly read about those concepts in the explanation of the learning goal and ask your trainer;
   - Read all the example questions you find in our explanation of the learning goals. Make sure you understand the answers.
3. (1-2 hours) To cross-check your understanding, skim through the glossary (Appendix B) and pay attention to terms you are less familiar with or that might be ambiguous. Terms that appear in the exam are used according to their definition in the glossary.
4. (1-2 hours) Test your knowledge with the mock exam that is available as a download from the iSAQB Github site, https://isaqb-org.github.io

Preparation in self-study

You can also choose to self-study for the examination, in which case we propose a four step process, allowing approximately 20 hours for this:

1. (15 minutes) Read the brief overview of the iSAQB curriculum (see section *iSAQB examination overview*).
2. (15 minutes) Skim through the list of learning goals (see introduction of Part II). If you encounter any terms you don't know - look them up in the glossary or read the explanation of the appropriate learning in Part II.
3. (4-16 hours) Read all the learning goals in detail (see introduction of Part II). Concentrate on the R1 relevance (as those will most likely be part of your examination). Mark all keywords or concepts you're unfamiliar with.
4. (1-2 hours) Read all the example questions you find in our explanation of the learning goals. Make sure you understand the answers.

5. (1-2 hours) To cross-check your understanding, skim through the glossary (see Appendix B) and pay attention to terms you are less familiar with, or that might be ambiguous. Terms that appear in the exam are used according to their definition in the glossary.

6. (1-2 hours) Test your knowledge with the mock exam that is available as a download from https://isaqb-org.github.io

Two things to keep in mind

1. You absolutely don't need to learn anything by heart. Please don't torture yourself by trying to memorize some ISO standard or the definitions of specific patterns and class diagrams, as this certainly won't help you in the examination!

2. A disclaimer: Any kind of preparation will improve your chances of succeeding, but it won't provide a guarantee. Neither training nor this book, despite it covering all learning goals, can make up for not possessing the essential prerequisites.

Part II: CPSA-F learning goals explained

Content overview
- How are learning goals (LGs) explained?
- List of all learning goals, structured according to the iSAQB Curriculum

How learning goals are explained

Every learning goal will be explained using the following structure:
- The learning goal (LG), often containing several learning-goal items;
- An explanation and background information, describing the intention and meaning of this LG; Likely, you will find definitions of important terms in this section;
- Exercises or sample questions concerning this LG;
- References to related LGs, related topics or other resources.

! Whenever you see a statement marked with a huge exclamation mark please note that this might be relevant for the examination.

List of learning goals

Please remember from the introduction: Learning goals marked with "R1" will be part of an examination, "R2" might be and "R3" will not be. Therefore, focus on the R1 and R2 learning goals when preparing for the examination.

The titles of the learning goals are slightly abbreviated here.

Nr	Learning goal	Relevance
LG 1-1	Definitions of software architecture	R1
LG 1-2	Goals and benefits of software architecture	R1
LG 1-3	Software architecture in the software lifecycle	R2
LG 1-4	Software architects' tasks and responsibilities	R1
LG 1-5	Relation of software architects to other stakeholders	R1
LG 1-6	Relation between development approaches and software architecture	R2
LG 1-7	Short- and long-term goals	R2
LG 1-8	Explicit statements versus implicit assumptions	R1

Nr	Learning goal	Relevance
LG 1-9	Responsibilities within the greater architectural context	R3
LG 1-10	Types of IT systems	R3
LG 1-11	Challenges of distributed systems	R3
LG 2-1	Approaches and heuristics for architecture development	R1, R3
LG 2-2	Design software architectures	R1
LG 2-3	Factors influencing software architecture	R1-R3
LG 2-4	Design and implement cross-cutting concepts	R1
LG 2-5	Architectural patterns	R1, R3
LG 2-6	Design principles	R1-R3
LG 2-7	Dependencies between building blocks	R1
LG 2-8	Achieve quality requirements	R1
LG 2-9	Design and define interfaces	R1-R3
LG 2-10	Principles of software deployment	R3
LG 3-1	Requirements of technical documentation	R1
LG 3-2	Describe and communicate software architectures	R1, R3
LG 3-3	Models and notations to describe software architecture	R2-R3
LG 3-4	Architectural views	R1
LG 3-5	Context view of systems	R1
LG 3-6	Document cross-cutting concepts	R2
LG 3-7	Describe interfaces	R1
LG 3-8	Document architectural decisions	R1-R2
LG 3-9	Additional resources and tools for documentation	R3
LG 4-1	Quality models and quality characteristics	R1
LG 4-2	Clarify quality requirements	R1
LG 4-3	Qualitative analysis	R2-R3
LG 4-4	Quantitative evaluation	R2
LG 5-1	Relation between requirements, constraints, and solutions	R3
LG 5-2	Rationale of a solution's technical implementation	R3

CPSA-F Chapter 1: Basic concepts of software architecture

LG 1-1: Definitions of software architecture

Discuss definitions of software architecture (R1)

Software architects know several definitions of software architecture (incl. ISO 42010/IEEE 1471, SEI, Booch, etc.) and can name their similarities:

- Components/building blocks with interfaces and relationships;
- Building blocks as a general term, components as a special form thereof;
- Structures, cross-cutting concepts, principles;
- Architecture decisions and their consequences on the entire system and its lifecycle.

1.1.1 Explanation

Our (personal) favorite among the many possible definitions of *software architecture* is provided by the IEEE 1471[9] standard:

Software architecture: the fundamental organization of a system embodied in its components, their relationships to each other and to the environment, and the principles guiding its design and evolution.

Let us explain some key terms of this definition:

Fundamental organization

The way things are ordered and each element is given its designated place. *Fundamental* because it must stand out clearly, be obvious to everyone who works on this system and act as the most profound guideline to be followed.

Components

The structural elements of software: Subsystems, modules, classes, functions - sometimes called *building blocks* (as a generic term). Components are usually implemented in source code in a programming language, but can also be other artifacts that (together) *make up the system.*

Relationships

Interfaces, dependencies, associations - many names for the same feature. Components need to interact with other components, otherwise no separation of concerns (division of responsibility) would be possible.

---

9 https://en.wikipedia.org/wiki/IEEE_1471

On the downside: Designing *good* interfaces is really difficult, and misunderstanding of interfaces is the source of many problems in software systems.

Environment
Every system has some relationships (aka interfaces, dependencies) to its environment: data, control flow or events are transferred to and from possibly different kinds of neighbors. The $\rightarrow$ context view of an IT system emphasizes the importance of these external interfaces.

Principles
A rule that holds for the whole system or several parts of it. Some decision, stipulation or definition, usually valid for several elements of the system. In this book we prefer the term *concept* instead of *principle*. Concepts are the foundation for $\rightarrow$ conceptual integrity or $\rightarrow$ consistency - in the authors' opinion one of the most important qualities of software systems.

Design and evolution
Cross-cutting and system-wide decisions might become necessary during both initial design and ongoing evolution and maintenance of systems. Most non-trivial systems require such decisions to be taken at key points during their lifecycle, definitely *not* restricted to the initial design and implementation phase.

! Make sure you know about the most important elements of any software architecture, namely *components* (building blocks of systems), *relationships* (dependencies, associations), the *environment* (all things outside of your system) and *principles* (cross-cutting topics or decisions). You should know that your *design or architecture decisions* might influence or relate to all of these elements.

Some more definitions
Let's look at a few of the definitions mentioned in this LG (you definitely don't need to remember the names and numbers of the ISO/IEEE standards or any authors' names).

! There are many different (valid) definitions of "software architecture".

ISO/IEC/IEEE 42010 definition of "architecture"
Fundamental concepts or properties of a system in its environment embodied in its elements, relationships, and in the principles of its design and evolution.

IEEE 1471 definition of "software architecture"
The fundamental organization of a system embodied in its components, their relationships to each other, and to the environment, and the principles guiding its design and evolution.

SEI / [Bass+2021] definition of "software architecture"

The software architecture of a system is the set of structures needed to reason about the system, which comprise software elements, relations among them, and properties of both.

Rational Unified Process (Booch, Kruchten et al.)

An architecture is the set of significant decisions about the organization of a software system, the selection of the structural elements and their interfaces by which the system is composed, together with their behavior as specified in the collaborations among those elements, the composition of these structural and behavioral elements into progressively larger subsystems, and the architectural style that guides this organization—these elements and their interfaces, their collaborations, and their composition.

Galan & Perry, 1996[10]

The structure of the components of a program/system, their interrelationships, and principles and guidelines governing their design and evolution over time.

Tom DeMarco [DeMarco1995]

An architecture is a framework for the disciplined introduction of change.

Eoin Woods[11]

Software architecture is the set of design decisions which, if made incorrectly, may cause your project to be canceled.

Commonalities of definitions

The following terms appear repeatedly in several definitions of *software architecture*:

- Component: Structural part or building block of systems.
- Structure: An arrangement of interrelated elements (aka. components or building blocks) that together perform a common task.
- Relationships / dependencies: The coupling of elements, enabling them to cooperate or exchange data.
- Design or architecture decisions: A system or its architecture evolves from an arbitrary number of (design or architecture) decisions of all kinds.
- Cross-cutting concepts / principles: Rules or heuristics valid at several locations or points throughout the system or its development.
- Decomposition of *larger* things into *smaller* things. One of the golden rules of life (and computer science): If a problem is too large to handle all at once, break it down into more manageable units.

---

10   https://www.cs.cmu.edu/afs/cs/project/able/ftp/saintro-tse95/saintro-tse95.pdf
11   http://www.softwarearchitectures.com/overview.html

1.1.2 Exercises

Name some common elements of software architecture definitions.

What kinds of things in your system might be influenced by architectural decisions?

A-question: How many definitions of *software architecture* exist in software engineering textbooks or standards?

Select the correct answer.

  [ ] One definition per category of IT system (e.g. embedded, real-time, decision-support, batch, mobile, web).

  [ ] One definition for all types of systems.

  [x] More than a dozen different definitions.

P-question: The term "software architecture" covers which of the following topics?

Select the three most appropriate.

  [ ] Relational database schema.

  [x] (Internal and external) interfaces.

  [x] Cross-cutting concepts ("principles").

  [ ] Hardware sizing.

  [x] Components ("building blocks").

1.1.3 References

- Software Engineering Institute collection of definitions, online: https://resources.sei.cmu.edu/asset_files/FactSheet/2010_010_001_513810.pdf
- Wikipedia on IEEE 1471, https://en.wikipedia.org/wiki/IEEE_1471
- Wikipedia on ISO 42010, https://en.wikipedia.org/wiki/ISO/IEC_42010

LG 1-2: Goals and benefits of software architecture

Understand and explain the goals and benefits of software architecture (R1)

Software architects can justify the following essential goals and benefits of software architecture:

- Support the design, implementation, maintenance, and operation of systems;
- Achieve functional requirements or ensure that they can be met;
- Achieve requirements such as reliability, maintainability, changeability, security, energy efficiency etc.;
- Ensure that the system's structures and concepts are understood by all relevant stakeholders;
- Systematically reduce complexity;
- Specify architecturally relevant guidelines for implementation and operation.

1.2.1 Explanation

In short: You need to know what software architecture (as a discipline, a role and an artifact) is good for!

Achieve quality

Some attributes (*qualities*) of a software system can only be achieved by taking *global* design decisions, spanning the context of several components or parts of the system.

Particularly in medium or large development teams, such qualities cannot be achieved by individual developers alone, but must be consistently *designed and incorporated into the system*.

Examples:
- High runtime performance can rarely be achieved by optimizing a single component alone.
- Maintainability of a system needs to be considered in every part of that system. It cannot be *added afterwards*.
- To ensure security (privacy, confidentiality) many different elements and aspects of system design, implementation and operation must be addressed adequately.

Facilitate development and maintenance

Systems should be constructed (*architected*) in such a way as to facilitate (simplify, ease) both development and maintenance. A reasonable set of design decisions should allow developers to be creative and productive, but on the other hand avoid disorder and chaos.

Beware of *overengineering* or *overarchitecting* your system. Usually you do *not* predefine or prescribe every little detail of every component or technical concept, but rather focus on *important* elements of the system.

Achieve consistency

The great Fred Brooks[12] said in 1975 that *"conceptual integrity is the most important consideration in system design"*.

Conceptual integrity means the design/architecture of a system follows a consistent set of rules or decisions (e.g. in UNIX mostly everything is a file, or in LISP everything is a list).

Conceptual integrity (or homogeneity or consistency, as we prefer to call it) is a necessary prerequisite for understandability and maintainability. It is a synonym for *appropriate standardization*, for deliberate, informed choices between design variants, and for the correct implementation of design decisions.

1.2.2 Exercises

P-question: What are the main goals of software architecture?

Select the two most appropriate answers.

[ ]   Improve pattern compliance in the structure and implementation of the system.

[x]   Achieve necessary quality requirements for the system in a comprehensible way.

[ ]   Enable cost-effective integration and acceptance testing of the system.

[x]   Provide the development team and other stakeholders with a basic understanding of the system's structures and concepts.

---

12   https://www.cs.unc.edu/~brooks/

LG 1-3: Software architecture in the software lifecycle

Understand software architecture as part of the software lifecycle (R2)

Software architects understand their tasks and can integrate their results into the overall lifecycle of IT systems. They can:

- Identify the consequences of changes in requirements, technologies, or the system environment in relation to software architecture;
- Elaborate on relationships between IT-systems and the supported business and operational processes.

1.3.1 Explanation

The design, evolution and degradation of a systems' architecture is interwoven with almost any part of the software lifecycle (SLC). While ISO/IEC/IEEE 12207:2017 [ISO-12207] describes a whole cornucopia of lifecycle processes that can be employed to define the lifecycle of a system, only some of them may be relevant to your *specific* IT system. Which ones depend on the particular system, its context and the development method used. However, most of them interact with the architecture of the system, albeit to varying degrees.

! Make sure to distinguish the software lifecycle (SLC) from the software development lifecycle
● (SDLC). The SLC is much broader in scope than the SDLC. Nevertheless, the tasks and responsibilities of software architects essentially cover almost the entire lifecycle of IT systems.

The software lifecycle

The software lifecycle describes all phases of a software product, starting with its planning, through its development and use, and ultimately its retirement. This process is rarely straightforward, but often involves iterations of sub-processes in which the IT system continues to evolve while older versions of it are gradually phased out. The widely cited *versioned staged model for the software lifecycle* by Rajlich and Bennett [Rajlich+2000] emphasizes the evolutionary nature of this process. It distinguishes the stages depicted in the figure below and characterizes them as follows (summarized from [Rajlich+2000]):

During *initial development*, the IT system and its architecture are designed and implemented from scratch. Architectural decisions are based on initial requirements and influencing factors, which are described in more detail in LG 2-3. At this stage architects and developers acquire knowledge of the application domain and the technologies used to implement the system, which will be crucial for its future development. More importantly, the architecture established at this stage will have a significant impact on the ease of future evolution. As an architect you have to be aware of management's interest in timely revenue generation and faster time to market that conflicts with investments that makes evolution easier and cheaper in the long run.

The *evolution* stage is characterized by iterative changes that originate in changing requirements, evolving technologies and lessons learned from the design and implementation process itself. Often the first release is not delivered after the initial development, but rather after several iterations during evolution, to ensure a better alignment with customer needs and a more stable system. Release dates are usually determined both by business considerations and by the degree to which quality requirements are met. This puts architects in a position where they have to broker a suitable trade-off between these, often conflicting, interests.

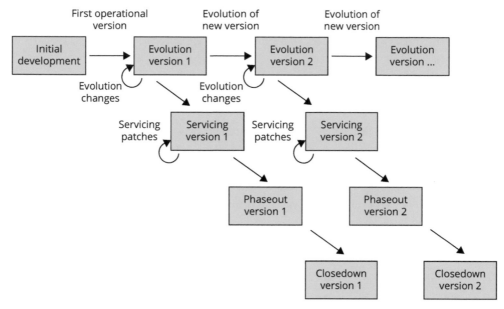

Figure 1.1 Versioned staged model for the software lifecycle by [Rajlich+2000]

Over time, changes accumulate to a point, where the software architecture of a system either loses its integrity and coherence or becomes an obstacle that limits future changes. This process might be accelerated by the loss of staff expertise. In order to facilitate further evolution, major changes to the system and its software architecture are required that must lead to the next version of the IT system if the software product is to be continued.

Once a system enters the *servicing* stage, there is usually no turning back and it is considered legacy. During servicing, changes are difficult and expensive. Therefore, they are performed in a way that minimizes cost and effort, leaving most of the underlying architectural problems untouched, thus leading to further decay and eventually *phaseout*. It's one of the architect's responsibilities to ensure that mission critical systems never end up in servicing, as management often does not understand or recognize the transition from evolution to servicing and might be caught out in the cold when needs for change can no longer be met.

During the *phaseout* stage, no more changes to the software are made and it becomes increasingly outdated. Customers and operations have to find workarounds for its deficiencies. As security issues increasingly mount and the system might, for instance, fail to satisfy changing regulatory standards, it becomes a liability rather than an asset.

Closedown marks the final end of the line for a particular version of a software system. Customers will be redirected to replacement systems. However, data migration and legal obligations like source code and data retention might still need to be considered.

! The terminology mentioned here, especially *evolution*, *servicing*, *phaseout* and *closedown*, are not relevant for the examination.

1.3.2 Exercises
- Reflect on the influence of software architecture decisions in the phases mentioned above. When has architecture the greatest or the least influence?
- Reflect on the consequences of changes in functional requirements to architecture decisions.
- Can a new or modified functional requirement have an impact on software architecture?

Think of examples:
- Reflect on the consequences of changes in quality requirements (see LG 4-2) on architecture decisions.
- Imagine that a single quality requirement (e.g. performance, robustness, understandability, etc.) is drastically changed. How might other quality attributes be affected by this?

1.3.3 References
- Influencing factors are covered in LG 2-3.

LG 1-4: Software architects' tasks and responsibilities

Understand software architects' tasks and responsibilities (R1)

Software architects are responsible for meeting requirements and creating the architecture design for a solution.

Depending on the actual approach or process model used, they must align this responsibility with the overall responsibilities of project management and/or other roles.

Tasks and responsibilities of software architects:

- Clarify and scrutinize requirements and constraints, and refine them if necessary, including *required features* and *required constraints*.
- Decide how to decompose the system into building blocks, while determining dependencies and interfaces between the building blocks.
- Determine and decide on cross-cutting concepts (for instance persistence, communication, GUI, etc.).
- Communicate and document the software architecture based on views, architectural patterns, cross-cutting and technical concepts.
- Accompany the realization and implementation of the architecture; integrate feedback from relevant stakeholders into the architecture if necessary; review and ensure the consistency of source code and software architecture.
- Analyze and evaluate software architecture, especially with respect to risks that involve meeting the requirements, see LG 4-3 and LG 4-4.
- Identify, highlight, and justify the consequences of architectural decisions to other stakeholders.

They should independently recognize the necessity of iterations in all tasks and point out possibilities for appropriate and relevant feedback.

1.4.1 Explanation

No algorithmic approach; iteration to the rescue

As software architecture design is a highly creative task, there is no *algorithmic* way for achieving results. See Part III "Appropriateness" on page 159.

Multiple factors influence architecture, design and implementation decisions: business and quality requirements, organizational and technical constraints, legal constraints, budget and time constraints, available technology, existing infrastructure, and many more.

It's rarely possible to have them all in mind at once.

As a natural consequence, iterative approaches with integrated feedback activities have become common in software development. You should be aware that an iterative approach does **not** necessarily mean Scrum or a similar method. Iterations can happen in all activities, even in waterfall-like development (although, of course, Agile projects are much better suited for getting feedback).

See also LG-1-6 (section on development approaches).

 Architecture needs feedback, therefore architecture work is inherently iterative.

Benefits of iterative-incremental approaches
- Early feedback;
- Early risk (and problem) identification;
- More time to fix problems and mitigate risks;
- Better chances to adapt to changes in requirements, constraints, technology, team etc.;
- Opportunities to practice every activity in the development process, especially deploy- and release-related activities.

Role and tasks of software architects
Software architecture is a team effort.

In our opinion, there should be one person in charge who can decide in case of doubt or if the team cannot easily come to a consensual decision.

Software architects (together with the development team) design and construct all elements that are necessary for the development, operation and maintenance of software systems:
- Building blocks as the structural elements of systems;
- Interfaces between building blocks or between external systems (neighbor systems);
- Cooperation of building blocks through interfaces;
- Cross-cutting concepts or rules;
- Selection of appropriate technologies;
- Adoption of suitable development and operation processes;
- Everything else that might be required to develop, implement, and operate the system.

Software architects need to fulfill six important tasks (depicted in Figure 1.2 below) in order to design and develop successful systems based upon given functional and quality requirements.

It always depends...
The order, intensity and duration of these activities is a system- and context- specific decision
- there is no general rule.

It's always a specific decision how much architecture, how much documentation, how much
communication, how much feedback and how much of everything else is needed in a specific
situation. See the section in Part III on *appropriateness* for additional considerations.

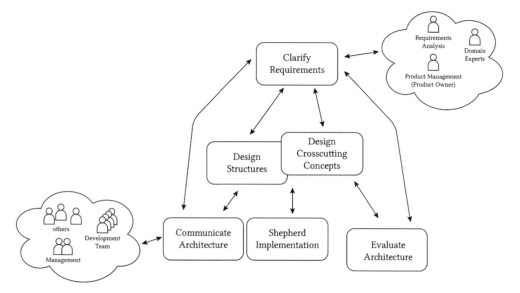

Figure 1.2 Six tasks of software architects

Clarify requirements

In (the likely) case of missing, unclear, inconsistent or contradictory requirements, software architects
need to actively clarify requirements in conjunction with the corresponding stakeholders.

We recommend clarifying the following:
- Who are the **stakeholders** of the system, in other words the roles or persons who are concerned
  about the system or its architecture, implementation, development, operation, deployment, main-
  tenance or the like.
- **Context and external interfaces**, expressing your system's relation to its communication partners
  (neighboring systems and users). Show and/or specify the external interfaces, usually to both other
  systems and user roles. See LG 3-5.
- **Quality requirements.** These often fundamentally influence architectural decisions. See LG 4-2.
- **Functional requirements**, see below.
- **Constraints** are facts/requirements/needs/limitations that *constrain* software architects in their
  freedom when making design and implementation decisions or decisions about the development
  process. See LG 2-3.

- **Stability, validity, and importance** of all the points above. Will a requirement still stand in two weeks, two months or two years? Is it something that was created on a whim, "because that's what everyone does", or is there a compelling reason behind it?

Clarify (relevant) functional requirements

Although you don't need to know the intricate details of *every single* functional requirement, you should have a good knowledge of the *architecturally relevant* ones, for example functions that:
- will be executed frequently;
- are the most important for your primary stakeholders;
- have critical timing or performance constraints;
- read, update, create or move large amounts of data;
- require critical parts of your infrastructure.

Design structures and concepts

Designing belongs to the primary tasks of software architects. In general, it means taking decisions and resolving potential conflicts between goals, requirements or constraints.

You should distinguish between two separate aspects of *designing*:
- Designing structures: → Structures are usually source code elements of arbitrary sizes, maybe subsystems, components, packages, name spaces or sometimes smaller elements like classes. We consider all kinds of building blocks relevant for structural design, in both white box and black box manifestations. Details are covered in LG 2-1 and LG 2-2.
- Designing (cross-cutting) concepts: → Concepts form the basis for → conceptual integrity (consistency, homogeneity) of the architecture. Thus, they are an important contribution to achieving the intrinsic qualities of your system. We call them cross-cutting as sometimes concepts cannot be handled by individual building blocks, but have to be applied to, or at, several architectural elements (e.g. security). Details are covered in LG 2-4.

Communicate architecture

Software architects need to communicate with various stakeholders about certain aspects of the system. Part of this communication involves argumentation, discussion and convincing people, other parts involve (written) documentation. Communicating the software architecture is addressed in Part 3 of the curriculum, especially sections LG 3-2, LG 3-3 and LG 3-9.

Shepherd implementation

In the end, the output of developers ultimately shapes how a system is built. Documenting architectural decisions (structures, concepts or other stuff) does not necessarily mean the system will be built according to that documentation. Things can and will go wrong. Software architects need to make sure the system is built in the appropriate way, decisions are properly implemented and architectural principles are adhered to. Shepherding the implementation is the key activity for achieving this:
- Identify those parts of the system and its implementation that violate or endanger *consistency* or somehow deviate from the chosen architecture. Together with the development team, find appropriate ways to correct or mitigate these issues.

- Identify potential design or implementation decisions which could improve the overall architecture. It's not at all uncommon to have good developers on your team who can come up with a simpler, clearer, cheaper or quicker solution, one less risky, more maintainable, requiring fewer resources to operate or inhibiting other kinds of improvements.

Evaluate architecture

Find out if (or if not) the system, its architecture and implementation can fulfill or satisfy its quality requirements or if any of these requirements are at risk. Basically "analyzing and evaluating" software seeks to assess the qualities of the system.

In this context we mean *product quality,* which is quite a complicated beast and is detailed further in LG 4-1: Quality is the set of desired or required attributes of a system, where different people might need or want different such attributes. For example: Some stakeholders want your system to be highly secure, whereas others want it to be highly usable, meaning that it is difficult (in some cases impossible!) to please both parties.

> In the context of software engineering, software quality refers to two related but distinct notions that exist wherever quality is defined in a business context:
> - Software functional quality reflects how well it complies with or conforms to a given design, based on functional requirements or specifications. This attribute can also be described as the fitness for purpose of a piece of software or how it compares to competitors in the marketplace as a worthwhile product.
> - Software structural quality refers to how it meets non-functional requirements that support the delivery of the functional requirements, such as robustness or maintainability, the degree to which the software was produced correctly. Source: Wikipedia[13].

In software architecture work it is mainly the second notion that we care for in order to guarantee the first notion over an extended period of time.

There are two main categories for architecture evaluation. Qualitative evaluation, which is covered in detail in sections LG 4-1, LG 4-2 and LG 4-3 and quantitative evaluation, detailed in LG 4-4.

1.4.2 Exercises

- Explain why it is often necessary or helpful to support requirements engineers or business analysts in clarifying requirements.
- Explain why some requirements (especially quality requirements) need to be prioritized. Consider potential contradictions or conflicts between such requirements.
- Name at least five different activities or approaches that could support your task of "shepherd implementation".

---

13 https://en.wikipedia.org/wiki/Software_quality

1.4.3 References

- See also LG-1-6 (the section on development approaches).
- "Design It!" [Keeling2017] by Michael Keeling is a pragmatic and yet systematic book on software architecture and the design activities within this role.
- [Cervantes+2016] gives a (sometimes quite academic) overview.

LG 1-5: Software architects and other stakeholders

Relate the role of software architects to other stakeholders (R1)

Software architects are able to explain their role. They should adapt their contribution to software development in a specific context and in relation to other stakeholders, in particular to:

- Product management and product owners;
- Project managers;
- Requirements engineers (requirements- or business analysts, requirements managers, system analysts, business owners, subject-matter experts, etc.);
- Developers;
- Quality assurance and testers;
- IT operators and administrators (applies primarily to production environments or data centers for information systems);
- Hardware developers;
- Enterprise architects and architecture board members.

1.5.1 Explanation

Regardless of the specific model or process of development, software architects need to be aware of the (potential) multitude of different → stakeholders who are relevant for a specific development.

In many cases, software architects will have at least the following four different *categories (types)* of stakeholders:

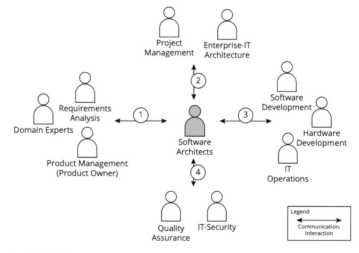

Figure 1.3 Categories of stakeholders

1. Stakeholders with a business-, product- or domain focus, e.g. product owner, requirements engineer or business analyst. With such people, architects often communicate on requirements and/or their feasibility, usually without using specific technical terminology.

2. Management stakeholders, like project management or enterprise IT management. With such people, architects communicate over organizational constraints, resources, schedules etc.
3. Technical stakeholders, like software- and/or hardware developers or IT-operations. With such people, architects usually communicate on a detailed and specific technical level.
4. Stakeholders focused on specific quality attributes, like IT-security or QA in general.

! ● Please beware that in your organization, there might be completely different stakeholders or stakeholder groups, and your specific needs of communicating with these might differ from the proposals given here.

As so often the rule 'it depends' (see Part III "Appropriateness" on page 159) applies here as well.

Collaboration with business and domain experts

Together with business and domain stakeholders or requirements engineering, software architects shall:

- clarify requirements;
- help identify conflicting requirements;
- support finding trade-offs between conflicting goals and requirements;
- explain the impact of certain requirements and constraints on other requirements, the architecture, implementation and operation of the system;
- support in prioritizing requirements and their development.

Collaboration with management stakeholders

Typical collaboration tasks between software architects and various management roles include:

- *technical consultancy*: architects are consulted by management concerning technical issues;
- *risk management*: architects point out and explain technical risks to management;
- support in *staffing*;
- support in defining and sizing work packages or work-breakdown-structures.

Collaboration with technical stakeholders

Within development teams, software architects shall:

- communicate and explain the architecture and architectural decisions;
- enable and prepare technical decisions;
- coach or help-to-coach team members;
- moderate in the discussion and design of internal and external interfaces.

! ● **Stakeholder-specific communication needed**
Many problems in software development cannot be solved by good programming alone, but need communication between stakeholders. A significant amount of such communication can be handled by software architects, who should be able to communicate in stakeholder-specific terminology, notation or level-of-detail.

1.5.2 Exercises

Reflect upon communication or stakeholder issues during your own software development experience:

- Think of problems that occurred when stakeholders from different groups needed to understand the technical consequences of their requests.
- Think of situations where the architect(s) needed to explain the consequences of business or quality requirements in relation to budget, schedule or risk.

1.5.3 References

Stakeholders play in important role in numerous other learning goals, e.g. LG 1-4, LG 1-6, LG 1-8, LG 3-1 and LG 3-2.

LG 1-6: Development approaches and software architecture

Can explain the correlation between development approaches and software architecture (R2)

- Software architects are able to explain the influence of iterative approaches on architectural decisions (with regard to risks and predictability).
- Due to inherent uncertainty, software architects often have to work and make decisions iteratively. To do so, they have to systematically obtain feedback from other stakeholders.

1.6.1 Explanation

As you have already seen in LG-1-4, architecture work needs feedback, which is an inherent feature of iterative development approaches. Due to their importance, let's repeat some crucial benefits of such approaches:

Benefits of iterative-incremental approaches

- Early feedback;
- Early risk (and problem) identification;
- More time to fix problems and mitigate risks;
- Better chances to adapt to changes in requirements, constraints, technology, team etc.;
- Opportunities to practice every activity in the development process, especially deploy- and release-related activities.

The fundamental ideas of iteration and regular feedback in engineering can be traced back to 1959[14], and have been widely known as the Deming-Cycle or *Plan-Do-Check-Adjust*, see the figure 1.4.

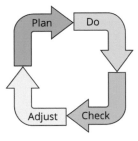

Figure 1.4 Plan-Do-Check-Adjust

A brief explanation:

- Plan: Make architectural decisions to meet the known/given requirements.
- Do: Execute this plan, implement these decisions.
- Check: Get feedback and evaluate the results from the *Do* phase.
- Adjust (sometimes called *Act*): Improve or refine decisions.

---

14 Deming, W. Edwards: Out of the Crisis, Cambridge, MA, 1986.

These four steps basically form the basis of every software development process. As a software architect, you should actively care for getting and giving sufficient and timely feedback (*push* and *pull*) from relevant stakeholders.

❗ Details of specific development approaches or processes will not be part of the examination.

1.6.2 Exercises

P-question: Why can iterative architecture and development approaches be helpful in software architecture?

Select the two most appropriate answers.

[ ]   In object-oriented systems, iteration can help reduce the coupling introduced by inheritance.

[x]   Short iterations can provide fast feedback on architectural decisions.

[ ]   Iteration cycles guarantee faster development.

[x]   Iteration cycles help to identify risks and problems earlier, providing more time to resolve them.

1.6.3 References

• See also LG-1-4 (the section on tasks and responsibilities).

LG 1-7: Short- and long-term goals

Differentiate between short- and long-term goals (R2)

Software architects can explain potential conflicts between short-term and long-term goals in order to find a suitable solution for all stakeholders.

Explanation

Usually project goals tend to be more short-term, whereas architecture goals tend to be long-term, as the life span of many software systems are much longer than the duration of typical development projects.

Let's clarify the term *project* and distinguish it from *system*.

Project

A *project* in software development or software-engineering is usually a collaborative effort to achieve clearly defined goals, in most cases within a limited time frame:

- Several people work together (*collaborate*);
- The outcome (*goal*) of their collaboration is clearly defined;
- The amount of time these people can invest is limited, as is the amount of money that can be spent during the project.

A person responsible for such a *project* will focus on the goals and outcomes of the project, and will likely not plan beyond the given time frame.

In day-to-day work, the term *project* is very often used synonymously with *system*, even though their meanings are very different!

For the purposes of this learning goal, you can even replace *Project* with *Sprint* if your organization uses Scrum as a development process.

System

The application, program, software or *thing* a development team is working on, which is usually the outcome of one or more *projects*.

A system may be defined as a set of components which accomplish a set of predetermined goals or fulfill predetermined requirements.

Usually the lifespan of a *system* is longer than it took to build that system - therefore goals related to that system are often long-term goals.

Short-term and long-term

- Projects typically last for a couple of weeks up to one or two years.
- Systems often remain in use for several years, larger systems in banking, insurance, telco or industry are often used 10+ years.

> **❗ Conclusion**
> - Project goals are often short-term;
> - Architecture or system goals are often long-term;
> - Architectural goals usually contribute to the achievement of project goals, but they can also be in conflict with each other.

Exercises

*K-question: Select which of the following statements regarding project goals and architectural goals are true and which are false.

True	False	
[x]	[ ]	Project goals can include functional requirements as well as quality requirements.
[x]	[ ]	Architectural goals are derived from the quality requirements of the system or product.
[ ]	[x]	Business stakeholders should concentrate on business goals and not interfere with architectural goals.
[ ]	[x]	To avoid conflicts, business goals and architectural goals should be non-overlapping sets.

Reflect on the following topics:

- Name a few typical short-term goals: What goals is your project manager aiming for?
- What factors influence short-term decisions more than others?
- In contrast, think of a few typical long-term goals, apart from maintainability of the system.
- Explain why neither of these types of goals (short- and long-term) should be called *better* than the other.

LG 1-8: Explicit statements versus implicit assumptions

Distinguish explicit statements and implicit assumptions (R1)

Software architects:

- Should explicitly present assumptions or prerequisites, therefore avoiding implicit assumptions;
- Know that implicit assumptions can lead to potential misunderstandings between stakeholders;
- Formulate implicitly, if it is appropriate in the given context.

1.8.1 Explanation

In our personal opinion, this is amongst the most important learning goals. Very often things go wrong due to different people having different implicit assumptions about something.

Software architects can and should be explicit in their decisions: Never call a decision *obvious*, as whilst it might be obvious to you, it might not be so obvious to others. It is better to explain (important) decisions explicitly, as this makes them easier to understand and avoids any misunderstandings.

 Prefer explicit statements over implicit assumptions.

When working in teams there's always the risk of misunderstanding unless we *explicitly* clarify things. This is often due to people making different assumptions.

We propose that you ensure explicitness in your work by, for example:

- Explicitly documenting quality requirements, e.g. in the form of quality scenarios;
- Explicitly documenting architecture decisions;
- Using clear and unambiguous terminology, especially domain/business terminology, e.g. by using an explicit domain model or a glossary for your system;
- Explicitly defining technical or cross-cutting concepts;
- Explicitly considering different perspectives before making difficult decisions, for example quality requirements, domain structure, external interfaces, building-block structure, technical infrastructure, etc.;
- Explicitly developing cross-cutting concepts to improve the → consistency → (*conceptual integrity*) of your system;
- Explicitly analyzing and evaluating your system, its architecture and code in order to get feedback on your architectural work;
- Explicitly asking stakeholders for feedback.

There will surely be additional aspects where *implicit assumptions* add risk to your work - and in your work as software architect you should always watch out for these dangers.

1.8.2 Exercises

- Think of at least three different situations where problems occurred in a development team due to *implicit assumptions*.
- How could these problems have been avoided?
- What facts, decisions or other things should have been made *explicit* in these cases?

K-question: You are developing the backend of a web-based information system. These backend services will be operated in a cloud environment and will be usable by every HTML5-enabled browser. Should the following topics be discussed or documented *explicitly*, or is it sufficient to know them *implicitly*?

Select the correct choice for each answer option.

explicitly	implicitly	
[ ]	[x]	Manufacturer of the mass storage, built into the cloud provider's data center.
[x]	[ ]	High priority quality requirements.
[ ]	[x]	Description of how a browser processes requests internally.
[x]	[ ]	Description of how your system handles network-communication failures.
[x]	[ ]	Reasons for major architectural decisions.

LG 1-9: Software architects in the greater architectural context

Responsibilities of software architects within the greater architectural context (R3)

The focus of the iSAQB CPSA Foundation Level is on the structures and concepts of individual software systems.

In addition, software architects are familiar with other architectural domains, for example:

- Enterprise IT architecture: structure of application landscapes;
- Business and process architecture: structure of, among other things, business processes;
- Information architecture: cross-system structure and use of information and data;
- Infrastructure or technology architecture: structure of the technical infrastructure, hardware, networks, etc.;
- Hardware or processor architecture (for hardware-related systems).

These architectural domains are not the content focus of CPSA-F.

1.9.1 Explanation

This learning goal is not relevant for the examination. However, you should be aware of other architectural domains.

Certain other *disciplines* (sometimes called *architectural domains*) also contain the term "architecture" in their names. Although concerned with decisions and structures for their specific domain, they differ from "software architecture" in many ways.

It might be helpful to have at least a basic understanding of these domains, so you can explain the differences to certain stakeholders within your organization, if required.

Enterprise IT architecture

Structure of the IT within the whole organization and description of IT-related processes, ranging from strategic planning, budgeting, vendor- and technology management, capability management and more.

Business architecture

Structure of the business itself, pertaining to organizational aspects, strategies and governance.

Process architecture

Sometimes called "business process architecture" - designing business processes. It is related to software and implementation aspects insofar as some of the processes to be supported by the software are defined here.

Information architecture

(from Wikipedia[15]) Information architecture is the structural design of shared information environments; the art and science of organizing and labelling web sites, intranets, online communities and software to support usability and findability; and an emerging community of practice focused on bringing the principles of design, architecture and information science to the digital landscape.

Hardware architecture

Design of (physical) devices, decisions about the hardware structure that an IT system relies on.

System architecture

Although (currently) not mentioned in the curriculum, we encounter this term quite often. *System architects* make decisions that affect the IT system as a whole, including hardware and software.

Please beware: The term "system" is heavily overloaded with numerous meanings and semantics, without a common understanding in IT. When somebody uses the term, please ask this person for the exact meaning in the given context!

1.9.2 Exercises

• Name some disciplines that also carry the term "architecture" in their names.
• Think of at least three definitions of the term "system" that you have encountered in practice.

—
15 https://en.wikipedia.org/wiki/Information_architecture

LG 1-10: Types of IT systems

Differentiate types of IT systems (R3)

Software architects know different types of IT systems, for example:

- Information systems;
- Decision support, data warehouse or business intelligence systems;
- Mobile systems;
- *Cloud native* systems;[16]
- Batch processes or systems;
- Systems based upon machine learning or artificial intelligence;
- Hardware-related systems; here they understand the necessity of hardware/software co-design (temporal and content-related dependencies of hardware and software design).

1.10.1 Explanation

Even if this learning goal is not relevant for the examination, you should know that different types or categories of IT systems can differ drastically in terms of their characteristics.

However, you should be aware of the fact that a vast variety of IT systems exist that can be categorized along multiple different "dimensions", comprising, but not limited to:

- Size and complexity (small, medium, large);
- Hardware dependency (system level driver, hardware independent middleware, application software);
- Degree of integration into hardware (embedded system);
- Online/offline operation;
- Volume and kind of data being processed (search-engine, data-warehouse, geometrical data, numerical data);
- Type of user interaction (keyboard or touch based, virtual-reality, graphical user interface, sensor/actor interfaces);
- Mobility or location-dependency (stationary, nomadic, mobile);
- Application domain (medical, automotive, finance, e-business. . .);
- Interaction with environment and timing constraints (reactive, interactive, transformative, batch-processing);
- Degree of specialization and intended distribution (customer specific solution vs. off-the-shelf application).

Although some of these dimensions may overlap, at least a rough classification is possible for most systems. This is significant to the extent that the fundamental requirements of the architecture and the development process can be derived from this classification. For example:

- When developing an embedded system, either the limitations of the hardware must be observed stringently or the development must be carried out in close cooperation with hardware designers.

---

16 [Cloud-Native]

- Reactive systems frequently have very demanding specifications regarding latencies and reaction times.
- When we develop a system for a specific customer, their particular and specific requirements can be identified and refined.
- When developing off-the-shelf solutions, development teams have to work with assumptions or marketing objectives.

1.10.2 Exercises

P-question: Can you identify examples of typical categories of software systems?

Choose the three most appropriate answers.

           [ ]   Linné's system.

           [x]   Batch system.

           [ ]   Integration test system.

           [x]   Interactive online system.

           [x]   Embedded real-time system.

LG 1-11: Distributed systems

Challenges of distributed systems (R3)

Software architects are able to:

- Identify distribution in a given software architecture;
- Analyze consistency criteria for a given business problem;
- Explain the causality of events in a distributed system.

Software architects know:

- Communication may fail in a distributed system;
- There are limitations regarding consistency in real-world databases;
- What the "split-brain" problem is and why it is difficult;
- That it is impossible to determine the temporal order of events in a distributed system.

1.11.1 Explanation

 This learning goal is not relevant for the examination.

You should know about challenges or issues with distributed systems, where parts of your system cooperate over networks and have to cope with latency, synchronization, consistency and other potential obstacles.

See [Tanenbaum+2016] for details on this difficult and advanced subject.

Distributed systems

The parts (*components*) of a distributed system are located on different parts of a network or on different computers. These parts communicate over the network. Three significant characteristics of distributed systems are:

- Concurrency of components: Components run independent of each other, on different computing nodes or machines, in different address spaces.
- Independent failure of components, making error handling or debugging difficult.
- No global clock, making consistency difficult: As no reference clock exists, no strict temporal order of events in a distributed system can be determined. Therefore it cannot be determined what happened in which order.

Typical problems in distributed systems

Also known as → *the fallacies of distributed computing*, several typical risks occur in distributed systems:

- High → latency caused by (potentially slow) network connections;
- Outages of nodes or components due to network connection issues;
- Bandwidth limitations can disrupt communication;

- Due to these risks, additional precautions for error handling and recovery are required, implying additional complexity.

Because handling these issues is really difficult, Martin Fowler formulated his *first rule of distributed systems*: Don't distribute[17].

1.11.2 References

Andrew Tanenbaum and Maarten van Steen maintain a free website, [Tanenbaum+2016], which discusses the challenges of distributed systems.

---

17 https://martinfowler.com/bliki/FirstLaw.html

CPSA-F Chapter 2: Design and development of software architectures

LG 2-1: Approaches and heuristics for architecture development

Select and use approaches and heuristics for architecture development (R1, R3)

Software architects are able to name, explain, and use the fundamental approaches of architecture development, for example:

- Top-down and bottom-up approaches to design (R1);
- View-based architecture development (R1);
- Iterative and incremental design (R1):
  - necessity of iterations, especially when decision-making is affected by uncertainties (R1);
  - necessity of feedback on design decisions (R1);
- Domain-driven design (R3);
- Evolutionary architecture (R3);
- Global analysis (R3);
- Model-driven architecture (R3).

2.1.1   Explanation

As there is no deterministic or algorithmic approach to software design, you should consider an iterative approach to designing your software and its architecture. These iterations exist in addition to the flow of the overall development process. That is, multiple iterations can take place within a certain software development step, or one single step of an architecture design iteration can span multiple software development steps.

Our suggestions for an effective architecture development methodology is to iterate over various methodical approaches. A few such approaches are shown in the diagram below.

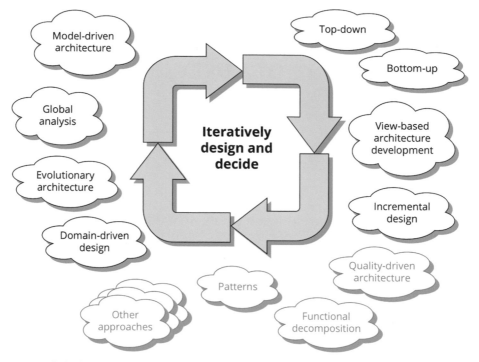

Figure 2.1 Methodical approaches to software design

Top-down approach

Start from a general, abstract or bird's eye perspective and step into details.

You may use a top-down approach within a single subsystem or component - this approach is not limited to the whole system.

For example, you could use a top-down approach to split the whole system into several subsystems, each of which will be developed by its own team.

Use a top-down approach to:
- Keep an overview of multiple components or subsystems;
- Abstract away details that are not currently needed;
- Keep things consistent over various components; or
- Work from abstract or large elements to specific or smaller ones.

Bottom-up approach

Think and work on a detailed level: Solve detailed problems, take detailed or low-level decisions. Later encapsulate (abstract away) these details, hiding them in higher-level abstractions, building blocks or components.

Use a bottom-up approach to:

- Reduce risks;
- Build proof-of-concept implementations;
- Validate decisions or proposals, proving that they can work in practice;
- Build-up knowledge and experience in important areas, like new technologies, products or business domains; or
- Work from detailed, specific or concrete elements up to larger, more abstract ones.

Top-down and bottom-up approaches complement each other nicely.

View-based architecture

Views focus on specific concerns, parts or aspects of a system. They can be used to consider certain things in isolation, thereby applying the "separation of concerns" principle to architecture work. Typical architecture views are covered in LG 3-4, with a preview shown in the diagram of Figure 2.2.

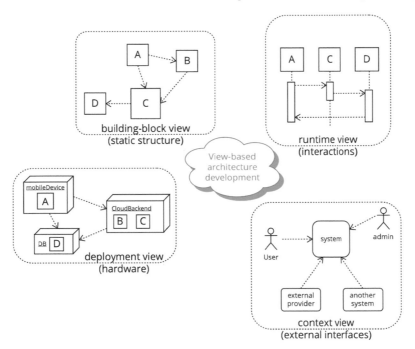

Figure 2.2 Typical architecture views

The context-, building block-, runtime- and deployment-view are often used in practice.

Use architecture views to:

- Facilitate structural, runtime or hardware decisions, as these concerns can be discussed separately;
- Facilitate communication and documentation;
- Gain flexibility in the degree of detail shown in various views; and
- Address specific stakeholder concerns (e.g. operational aspects are covered in the deployment view).

Iterative and incremental design

The combination of iterative and incremental work has been suggested for software development by numerous sources, and is widely accepted in IT. See [Larman+2003].

To understand the benefits of this combination, we need to clarify both constituents:
- Iterative: The system is constructed and built in repeated cycles (iterations). Each iteration delivers or improves part of the required system. Within iterations it's recommended to make appropriate design modifications parallel to adding new capabilities or functions to the system. After each iteration, feedback from participating stakeholders concerning the delivered work, the development and the overall process is collected. *Learning* and *improvement* is based upon this feedback.
- Incremental: Work is done in pieces, building upon each other. Each increment delivers a slice of functionality through cross-discipline work, from requirements over architecture/design, implementation through to deployment.

Combining both approaches allows development teams to capitalize on lessons learned earlier and deliver working software with each iteration/enhancement.

Major advantages of this combined approach include:
- Problems are detected early, allowing more time to resolve them
- Typical development and rollout activities are performed in every iteration, leading to routine processes and less errors
- Changes in requirements or technologies can be taken into account
- Development risks and uncertainties are minimized.

Domain-driven design (DDD)

Domain-driven design (the term was coined by Eric Evans in 2003) is an approach to developing software for complex application domains by connecting the implementation of an IT system to a flexibly evolving model of the core business concepts.

It facilitates a common understanding of the important business terminology between development teams and business people by creating a common (ubiquitous) language used by both of these groups.

Development teams then turn what is described in this ubiquitous language into code.

In the seminal book [Evans-2003] the author proposes two approaches that should both be used:
- *Strategic design*, structuring the business into subdomains and business-driven partitions he calls *bounded contexts*. This strategic design is a typical top-down approach.
- *Tactical design*, identifying events, services, entities + value objects (data). In contrast to strategic design, this is relatively low-level and a typical bottom-up approach.

From our personal experience, DDD integrates quite well with the microservice architecture pattern, covered in LG 2-5.

Evolutionary architecture

The term "evolutionary architecture" has been coined by [Ford+2017].

This approach allows guided, incremental change within architectures, based upon the notion of -> *fitness functions*.

Such a fitness function is composed of measurements from manual evaluations and automated tests, quantifying to what extent architectural or quality requirements (like performance or correctness) have been met:

> *Performance requirements make good use of fitness functions. Consider a requirement that all service calls must respond within 100ms. We can implement a test (i.e., fitness function) that measures the response to a service request and fails if the result is greater than 100ms. To this end, every new service should have a corresponding performance test added to the suite.*

[Ford+2017], Chapter 2.

This approach combines the concept of "global analysis" (see below) with executable specifications, making it very developer-friendly and applicable.

As some quality requirements like security, usability or legal requirements are hard if not impossible to test automatically, the authors of this method propose to use *manual fitness functions* instead: The primary aspect is to make the notion of quality explicit.

Global analysis

Created by a group of software architects from the medical domain that successfully built several safety-critical systems (see [Hofmeister+1999]), global analysis is a systematic approach to achieving desired quality attributes and considering existing constraints.

Global analysis starts by identifying and describing the factors which could affect the architecture. It then builds strategies which foresee and acknowledge the potential consequences of these factors.

Additional approaches

A few different approaches are not mentioned in this learning goal, but might still be interesting or useful in practice.

This list is by no means complete, there will be other methodical approaches to software design not covered here (that's what we mean by "other approaches" in the lower left corner of Figure 2.1).

Patterns

You could re-use existing solution approaches, especially architectural *patterns*. Several important patterns are covered in LG 2-5.

Quality-driven software architecture

For each required quality scenario (see LG 4-2), identify concrete sets of actions or steps to achieve it. This approach has been derived from *global analysis* (see above). It has many similarities to evolutionary architecture (see section earlier in this chapter).

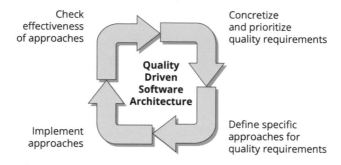

Figure 2.3 QDSA approach

It's a very simple, iterative and intuitive process, as shown in Figure 2.3:

1. Concretize and prioritize the necessary quality requirements.
2. Plan measures: Define (together with your team) measures or approaches for the respective quality requirements.
3. Implement the highly prioritized approaches.
4. Check the effectiveness of your approaches. You need to measure and test the running system or parts of it.
5. Continue with step 1.

This iterative procedure systematically checks the achievement of the important quality requirements of the system. It ensures that high-priority quality requirements are taken into account within architecture and development.

Functional decomposition

Take design decisions along the required functions, activities or processes of the system. Break down the overall function of the system into smaller parts.

One approach to achieve functional decomposition starts while *clarifying requirements* (see LG 1-4): You can sort, group or cluster functional requirements into groups that have high functional or business cohesion ("belong together"). Implement each of these functional clusters in its own component or module.

2.1.2 Exercises

K-question: For each of the following statements decide whether it is true or false.

Select the correct choice for each answer option.

true	false	
[ ]	[x]	The total effort spent on architectural work is much higher in iterative projects compared to waterfall projects.
[ ]	[x]	Iterative development does not need architecture documents since the development team uses daily standup-meetings to communicate decisions.
[x]	[ ]	Iterative and incremental development can help to reduce development risks.
[ ]	[x]	Important architectural decisions should be taken prior to the first iteration.

2.1.3 References

- Domain-driven design (DDD):
  - extensively covered by [Evans-2003];
  - a pragmatic and hands-on coverage by Michael Plöd, https://leanpub.com/ddd-by-example;
  - a large community evolved around this method, https://dddcommunity.org;
- Evolutionary architecture, see [Ford+2017];
- Global analysis, see [Hofmeister+1999]. For a short overview, see http://thesis.msc-cse.com/pdf/article_globalanalysis.pdf.
- View-based architecture:
  - LG 2-2 covers architecture views and their application;
  - LG 3-4 covers how architecture views can be used for communication and documentation;
  - The pragmatic software architecture template arc42 (see https://arc42.org) makes heavy use of different views;
  - See [Clements+2010] et al., on documenting architectures using views;
- Patterns see LG 2-5;
- Quality-driven architecture, https://www.innoq.com/en/articles/2012/04/quality-driven-software-architecture/ (in German).
- In the Software-Engineering Radio Podcast, Professor Marco Faella discusses different 'qualities' of code: https://www.se-radio.net/2020/10/episode-430-marco-faella-on-seriously-good-software/

LG 2-2: Design software architectures

Design software architectures (R1)

Software architects are able to:

- Design and appropriately communicate and document software architectures based upon known functional and quality requirements for software systems that are neither safety- nor business-critical;
- Make structurally-relevant decisions regarding system decomposition and building-block structure, and deliberately design dependencies between building blocks;
- Recognize and justify the interdependencies and trade-offs of design decisions;
- Explain the terms *black box* and *white box* and apply them purposefully;
- Apply stepwise refinement and specify building blocks;
- Design architecture views, especially building-block view, runtime view and deployment view;
- Explain the consequences of these decisions on the corresponding source code;
- Separate technical and domain-related elements of architectures and justify these decisions;
- Identify risks related to architecture decisions.

2.2.1 Explanation

Sidenote: This learning goal explicitly excludes safety- and business-critical systems, the reason being simply that the iSAQB does not want to be sued in case of failure.

Design and communicate software architectures

Software architects need to (1) take design decisions and (2) communicate these. That sounds simple, but these two activities can be difficult:

- Designing belongs to the core task of the architecture role (see below). It involves taking decisions that are *pro* certain options (like structures, interfaces or technologies), but also *against* (contra) others. To design and decide, you need to take into account at least the following factors:
  - requirements and constraints;
  - available components, technologies or other elements;
  - available skills in the development team;
  - potential conflicts between goals, requirements or constraints.
- To communicate such decisions and options might involve conquering resistance, identifying proper arguments for the pros and cons, finding the right language or communication media to reach out to other people, balancing written and verbal communication and other challenges.

Structural decisions

A structure (in most general terms) consists of structural elements and their dependencies. In Figure 2.4 the internal structure of `Something` is shown: it consists of `Element 1` to `Element 3` plus the dependencies `d1` to `d3`. This structure shows the *composition* of `Something` from constituent parts. In other words: `Something` is made up from its elements `Element 1`, `Element 2` and `Element 3` plus their dependencies or relations.

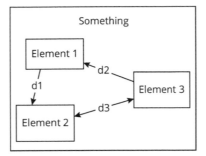

Figure 2.4 Example of a general structure

In software architecture, the structural[18] elements of a system are the source code artifacts, plus pre-compiled libraries, frameworks, files or similar things. We propose to use the general term *building blocks* for such elements. Building blocks may have more specific categories, like subsystems, parts, components, packages, namespaces or sometimes smaller elements such as classes, functions, configuration-files or similar. They can be of arbitrary size, small or large.

Building blocks: black box and white box

"Building block" (or the abbreviated term *block*) is the most general term for all kinds of artifacts from which software is constructed.

Building blocks and dependencies are the constituents of structural design, as explained above.

We can treat or regard every building block as both white box and black box:
- A black box hides the interior structure, whereas the
- white box shows the interior structure of a building block.

In Figure 2.5 you will see two building blocks, `Something` and `SomethingElse`, both displayed as white boxes. They both show their contained building-blocks ('`Element 1`', '`Part-A`' etc.) plus their dependencies. These contained building-blocks are mostly black boxes that hide their interiors, with the exception of `Part-W`, which is also a white box.

---

18 To be exact, building-blocks are parts of the *static* structure of systems, in contrast to e.g. *dynamic* or *deployment* structures.

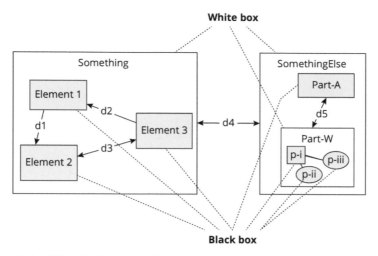

Figure 2.5 'Something' and 'SomethingElse' as white box

These different representations of a building block (black box and white box) can be immensely useful for software architecture. Both black and white boxes are representations of building blocks. A single building block can be a black box in one communication, diagram or model, and a white box in others.

Properties of black box representations

As a black box hides internal structure, it adheres to the →information hiding principle. Hiding internal things is an abstraction or simplification. When using the black box representation or simply the name of a building block, one does not need to consider all the internal details. This abstraction can simplify communication or documentation.

In addition, you might use a black box to delegate responsibility for the design and implementation of this building block to somebody else.

> **!** A black box hides:
> - Internal structure, that means internal building blocks and internal dependencies;
> - Internal processing, algorithms or functions;
> - Internal data and data structures.

A black box should have an appropriate name[19], and needs to expose the following in its description (black box template):
- Its responsibility: what does this black box do, what is its function or service?
- The *provided* interface(s): what functions, services or data does this black box provide?
- The *required* interface(s): what other functions, services or data does this black box require to fulfill its responsibility?

---

19 Finding good names is a serious problem in software development, and lots of online resources address this problem. See for example https://hilton.org.uk/blog/why-naming-things-is-hard

In some cases it can be useful if a black box provides some additional information about itself:

- Additional attributes, like qualities: Is this black box capable of multi-user access, what is the maximum throughput, what are guaranteed, minimal or average response times and so on.
- Known restrictions, risks or problems.

Properties of white box representations

As a white box is the "same thing" as its black box, it inherits all attributes of the black box, and adds the internal structure. In addition, we propose that a white box representation explains the reason why it is structured exactly in this specific way, sometimes called the → *design rationale.*

To summarize, a white box representation of a building block should contain the following information (white box template):

- Name of this white box;
- Reference or link to its black box;
- An overview (at best a diagram) of its internal structure, showing the contained black boxes plus their dependencies;
- *Design rationale*, the reason for this structure;
- A list or table of contained black boxes, each with name, responsibility and dependencies.

Decomposition by changing from black box to white box

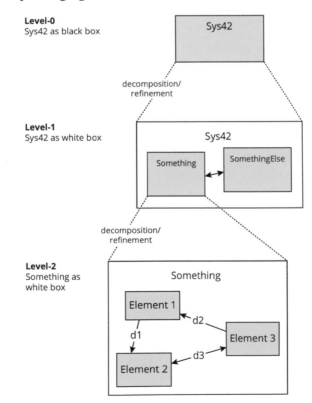

Figure 2.6 Decomposition/refinement

A fundamental concept of the building-block view in software architecture (see LG 3-4) is the systematic on-demand refinement of black boxes to white boxes in order to increase levels of detail.

Consider a system (`Sys42`) which consists of two building blocks (`Something` and `SomethingElse`), as depicted in Figure 2.6. On the topmost (abstraction) level (level 0), the system is depicted as a black box. On the next refinement level (level 1) `Sys42` is decomposed into the two black boxes `Something` and `SomethingElse`. Another refinement converts `Something` into a white box, showing its internal structure.

This is a simple method to explain the static structure of any software system by starting at the context level, and applying stepwise refinement. This approach is the underlying idea of the building-block view (see LG 3-4).

Such stepwise refinement serves two different purposes: firstly it is a communication mechanism, facilitating understanding of low-level structures by showing these structures in context. And secondly, you may start designing and implementing your system on any abstraction level and use a combination of bottom-up and top-down approaches (see LG 2-1) during development.

Recognize interdependencies and trade-offs between design decisions

Many decisions will have consequences - and you will not get any advantage *for free*. Often these consequences are hidden or indirect, but they might be grave.

Practicing sports several times per week might improve your health, but will reduce the time you can spend with your family. Learning a new programming language intensively will reduce the time you can spend on other activities. Adding several runtime configuration options to your software will make it more flexible for users to adjust to their specific needs, but will increase your test effort.

The popular saying *there ain't no such thing as a free lunch* (TANSTAAFL[20]) is used in economics and other disciplines to drive this point home. In software architecture and system development you should be aware of it and consider its consequences.

Some examples:
- Great runtime performance (*good*) often created by caching, parallel execution, sophisticated pre-loading strategies and such, quite often increases code size and complexity (*bad*).
- Excellent usability, attractive user interfaces and great user experience (*good*) require sophisticated UI- and UX- design efforts. This is potentially more costly (*bad*) than a rudimentary UI.
- Explicit data consent policies (where users always have the choice whether to allow access to specific kinds of their data) increase data privacy (*good*), but require many additional choices by users, making a system slightly more complicated to use (*bad*).

---

20 https://en.wikipedia.org/wiki/There_ain%27t_no_such_thing_as_a_free_lunch

Stepwise refinement

One option for designing software and other systems is stepwise refinement. In LG 2-1 we covered the *top-down* approach for the design process - basically another term for stepwise refinement. You start with the overall system or a part of it and break it down into parts (building blocks, components, subsystems). Next, you take one of these parts and break that one down into even smaller parts (building blocks).

Looking again at Figure 2.6, you can see two such refinement steps.

Using stepwise refinement is one approach to identifying or designing the building blocks of a system.

Design architecture views

Using different views on systems is an established practice in several engineering disciplines. For example, construction companies utilize floor plans and elevation plans, electrical and heating plans as well as escape and rescue plans, to name just a few well-known views from this particular domain.

In software architecture, the concept of different views has been extensively published and used in practice (e.g. [Kruchten1995], [Rozanski+2011] or [arc42]). LG 2-1 introduced four important views for software systems which will be covered in detail in LG 3-4 and LG 3-5.

Taking different views on the same system is an effective means of reasoning about the consequences of certain decisions. For example, comparing the runtime- and the building block view of a system might help to identify overly high coupling or bad cohesion.

! Architecture views support both designing and communicating architectures. Therefore they are more than just a means for documentation!

Relation of building blocks to source code

Ultimately, all building blocks will be implemented in source code. In some cases, your own development team will implement all your building blocks. In other cases, you may buy or use building blocks implemented by others.

To consider the general relation of building blocks to source code, we need to distinguish between white box and black box again.

The source code of:
- Any white box consists of *all* the source code of its contained black boxes.
- A *small* black box might consist of a single file, class or function definition in the appropriate programming language.
- A larger black box (like `Something` in the example above) consists of the source code of all contained elements. Although the contained elements are not exposed in the black box representation of a building block, they are nevertheless *contained* within this black box.

Please note: Building blocks do not necessarily represent single files or directories within a file system or version control system. The source code of a single building block might be spread over several files or folders, although that could be confusing.

Separate technical aspects from domain-related elements

The (SoC) principle (detailed in LG 2-6) proposes to separate responsibilities.

If domain-related elements of a systems are coupled to purely technical details (like file names, specific database names etc.), they become more difficult to understand, change or test.

Another aspect, which is also covered in LG 2-6, is *cohesion*: Aspects that belong together should be brought together - especially in building blocks.

Identify risks related to architectural decisions

Some architectural decisions involve → tradeoffs, see above in this section. Trading off one attribute or quality against another might be a risk or problem for some stakeholders, and you should consider and communicate such → risks.

Other decisions might contain risks due to a variety of reasons, e.g.:
• The proposed approach is highly innovative and has not been thoroughly evaluated or tested as yet.
• People involved in implementing the approach lack the required experience, but nobody else is available for the task.
• Technologies used in an approach have not been used in that specific combination before, and could not be tested in advance.
• You already know the solution is suboptimal, but the resources required for a better solution are not available (e.g. money, people, technology).
• You or the development team have been (e.g. organizationally) forced into a specific solution approach, which has caused problems in other systems or organizations.

> There are many more reasons that decisions could be deemed risky. We consider it your task to identify and communicate risks to other stakeholders, especially management and business.

2.2.2 Exercises

P-question: Which architecture views are used in software development?

Select the two most appropriate answers.

      [ ]   Pattern view.

      [x]   Building block (or component) view.

      [ ]   Linné's view.

      [x]   Deployment view.

See also LG 3-3.

K-question: Should the following characteristics of building blocks be described in its *black box* representation?

Select the correct choice for each answer option.

true	false	
[ ]	[x]	Algorithms used in implementation.
[x]	[ ]	Public interface(s).
[x]	[ ]	Outgoing interface(s).
[ ]	[x]	Internal performance optimization strategy.
[ ]	[x]	Internal implementation structure.
[x]	[ ]	Responsibility of this building block.
[ ]	[x]	Patterns used in implementation.

Reflect on potential (negative) consequences of the following decisions:

- You optimize runtime performance of database queries by implementing sophisticated pre-loading and caching.
- You create many (say, hundreds of) additional automated test cases, so potential bugs and regressions are caught early.
- You increase security by encrypting data within your database, and aggressively minimize the time this data is available in a decrypted state within the system.

2.2.3 References

Please see the references in LG 2-1.

LG 2-3: Influencing factors and constraints

Identify and consider factors influencing software architecture (R1-R3)

Software architects are able to clarify and consider requirements (including constraints that restrict their decisions). They understand that their decisions can lead to additional requirements (including constraints) on the system being designed, its architecture, or the development process.

They should recognize and account for the impact of:
- **Product-related** requirements such as (R1):
  - functional requirements;
  - quality requirements;
- **Technological** constraints such as:
  - existing or planned hardware and software infrastructure (R1);
  - technological constraints on data structures and interfaces (R2);
  - reference architectures, libraries, components, and frameworks (R1);
  - programming languages (R2).
- **Organizational** constraints such as:
  - organizational structure of the development team and of the customer (R1), in particular Conway's law (R2).
  - company and team cultures (R3);
  - partnerships and cooperation agreements (R2);
  - standards, guidelines, and process models (e.g. approval and release processes) (R2);
  - available resources like budget, time, and staff (R1);
  - availability, skill set, and commitment of staff (R1).
- **Regulatory** constraints such as (R2):
  - local and international legal constraints;
  - contract and liability issues;
  - data protection and privacy laws;
  - compliance issues or obligations to provide burden of proof.
- **Trends** such as (R3):
  - market trends;
  - technology trends (e.g. blockchain, microservices);
  - methodology trends (e.g. Agile);
  - (potential) impact of further stakeholder concerns and mandated design decisions.

Software architects are able to describe how those factors can influence design decisions and can elaborate on the consequences of changing influencing factors by providing examples for some of them (R2).

2.3.1 Explanation
Impact of quality requirements

Quality requirements (see LG 4-1 and LG 4-2) have a major influence on many architectural decisions.

Consider the following examples: Imagine the functional requirement "store and retrieve digital photos". A digital photo is just a rectangle of pixels, each represented by a numeric color value. You would need to add some metadata, like camera type, location and a few others. From an implementation perspective, that's a simple requirement.

Now let's add two different (hypothetical) quality requirements:

1. Your application is supposed to store approximately 100,000 of such images, but each image contains secrets that need to be protected. This is a security requirement - and you now need to take account of IT-security issues like encrypted persistence, restricted access to only certain users, password recovery policies and a few other critical topics.
2. Your application needs to handle images for up to 100 million people - and every one of them can store an arbitrary number of images. Now you have to deal with storage capacity and volume, transfer costs, backup performance, etc.

For both quality requirements, the architectural decisions will certainly differ from naive solutions based solely upon the (simple) functional requirements.

> **i** A practical example of the influence of quality requirements can be found in the well-known social-media service Twitter. An implementation of a short-message service with users that can subscribe to each other and post messages is rather simple - Github lists more than 200 of such systems[21]. If you add real-world performance, throughput and latency requirements, things become a lot more complicated.

Impact of technical decisions and constraints

A technical constraint can have a substantial impact on your architectural decisions. Again, let's consider some examples:

1. Database and persistence technology need to be provided by a specific vendor that only offers a relational database system, which only runs on a specific proprietary operating system. As an architect, you are now restricted in your decisions on how to store and retrieve data.
2. Your software is supposed to run on a specific GPU (graphics processing unit). Such GPU's are the core component of modern graphic cards and make use of a high degree of parallelism. As an architect, you are now restricted to programming environments and libraries that are available for your specific brand or type of GPU. You will need highly specific development and debugging tools, and many *standard programming tasks* will have to be implemented very differently on your GPU hardware.

---

21 See https://github.com/topics/twitter-clone

ⓘ In our practical experience we have encountered many technical constraints, usually in larger organizations striving for architecture and infrastructure standardization. Such constraints can be really helpful (there might be a lot of know-how available concerning the specific technology within the organization). Or they can be a real nuisance (the technology prescribed is old, outdated or deprecated). As always, it depends.

Impact of organizational constraints

The organizational structure can and will influence software architecture. This typical impact was initially noted by Melvin Edward Conway and later quoted as "Conway's Law", although it is a sociological observation:

> *Any organization that designs a system (defined broadly) will produce a design whose structure is a copy of the organization's communication structure.*

Melvin E. Conway, 1968 https://www.melconway.com/Home/Conways_Law.html

Conway's law is a specific adage that addresses organizational factors. Often there is no technological or business reason why certain functionalities that actually belong together are implemented by different subsystems. It "just happened somehow" during design and implementation. (Of course not, there is a socio-dynamic reason behind it.) This can be a serious problem, as it might degrade desirable properties of the architecture or be an additional source of errors. Since this unintended separation into subcomponents can (and will) occur in practice, you should be aware of it. Some organizations apply the "Inverse Conway Maneuver" to structure teams along architectural building blocks to prevent this from happening by chance.

2.3.2 Exercises

Review the factors listed in the learning goal description and find examples of how each of these factors has influenced architectural decisions in your projects in the past.

What effect did, or could, changes have to these factors?

P-question: Which factors do in general have the most influence on the design of software architectures?

Select the three most appropriate answers.

     [ ]   Virtual reality.

     [x]   Data privacy regulations.

     [x]   Organizational.

     [ ]   Ethical.

     [x]   Technical.

Remark: Although ethical factors can (and sometimes should) influence design decisions, in most cases their influence is less pronounced than that of other factors.

P-question: Which of the following requirements must be met before creating or developing a software architecture.

Select the two most appropriate.

[ ]   All requirements are provided in a complete, detailed and consistent manner.

[x]   The most important quality requirements are known.

[x]   Organizational constraints and conditions are known.

[ ]   The programming language has been selected.

[ ]   Hardware for the development team has been provided.

2.3.3 References

- Clarification and specification of quality requirements: See LG 4-2.
- Quality models and quality characteristics: See LG 4-1.
- The impact of organizational constraints on architecture ("Conway's Law") has been discussed, particularly in the context of microservices.
  See for example https://microservices.io or https://samnewman.io.

LG 2-4: Cross-cutting concepts

Design and implement cross-cutting concepts (R1)

Software architects are able to:

- Explain the significance of such cross-cutting concepts;
- Decide on and design cross-cutting concepts, for example persistence, communication, GUI, error handling, concurrency, energy efficiency;
- Identify and assess potential interdependencies between these decisions.

Software architects know that such cross-cutting concepts may be re-used throughout the system.

2.4.1 Explanation

Some architectural decisions will concern or affect topics relevant for multiple or all elements within the architecture. A typical (though low-level) example is *logging*, another example are security-related topics, see Figure 2.7.

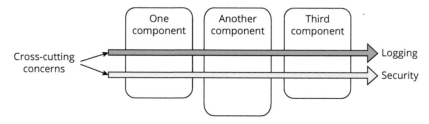

Figure 2.7 Cross-cutting concerns

Such concepts include overarching or cross-cutting issues, which often affect several building blocks of the system. These concepts can have a significant impact on the building block structures or their implementation. They often represent central technical decisions.

Cross-cutting concepts can be used to solve *recurring* problems (aka cross-cutting *concerns*) that have to be addressed within multiple elements of the architecture (see the *logging* example above - logging has to be done in all components or building blocks).

Some examples of such cross-cutting concerns are:

- Fundamental technology decisions relevant throughout the system or within several building blocks;
- Selection of frameworks or third-party tools/libraries;
- Usage of such technologies within the system, or for specific purposes;
- Conventions for interfaces between building blocks.

Significance of cross-cutting concepts

Cross-cutting decisions can help to ensure *consistency*: Topics governed by cross-cutting concerns will (most likely) be implemented in the same manner, based upon the same technology, using the same patterns or conventions.

Such consistency facilitates understanding and makes the corresponding parts or elements of the system *similar* in these specific aspects.

Often such concepts are used for knowledge-transfer between people and/or systems. A concept that has helped solve a specific problem in one system might be re-used in another system.

Risks involved in cross-cutting concepts

Similar to every standardization effort: If the standard is bad, systems using the standard will (likely) also be bad. If your cross-cutting concepts do not solve the underlying problems, then all components using or implementing those concepts will have issues.

2.4.2 Exercises

Q: Select the three most appropriate of the following statements about (cross-cutting) concepts.

[ ]   Uniform usage of concepts reduces coupling between building blocks.

[ ]   The definition of appropriate concepts ensures the pattern compliance of the architecture.

[ ]   For each use case there should be an explicitly documented concept.

[X]   Concepts are a means to increase consistency.

[X]   A concept can define constraints for the implementation of several building blocks.

[X]   A concept might be implemented by a single building block.

2.4.3 References

LG 3-6 also deals with cross-cutting concepts.

LG 2-5: Patterns

Describe, explain and appropriately apply important solution patterns (R1, R3)
Software architects know:
- Various architectural patterns and can apply them when appropriate;
- That patterns are a way to achieve certain qualities for given problems and requirements within given contexts;
- That various categories of patterns exist (R3);
- Additional sources for patterns related to their specific technical or application domain (R3).

Software architects can explain and provide examples for the following patterns (R1):
- *Layers*:
    - abstraction layers hide details, example: ISO/OSI network layers, or "hardware abstraction layer". See https://en.wikipedia.org/wiki/Hardware_abstraction ;
    - another interpretation are layers used to (physically) separate functionality or responsibility. See https://en.wikipedia.org/wiki/Multitier_architecture ;
- *Pipes-and-filters*: Representative for data flow patterns, breaking down stepwise processing into a series of processing-activities ("filters") and associated data transport/buffering capabilities ("pipes");
- *Microservices* split applications into separate executables that communicate via a network;
- *Dependency injection* as a possible solution for the dependency-inversion-principle [Newman2015].

Software architects can explain several of the following patterns, explain their relevance for concrete systems, and provide examples (R3): blackboard, broker, combinator, CQRS (Command-Query-Responsibility-Segregation), event-sourcing, interpreter, integration and messaging patterns, the MVC family of patterns (like MVC, MVVM, MV-Update, PAC), interfacing-patterns (like adapter, facade, proxy), observer, plug-In, Ports&Adapters (syn. onion-architecture, hexagonal-architecture), remote procedure call, SOA (service-oriented architecture), template, strategy, visitor.

Software architects know essential sources for architectural patterns, such as POSA [Buschmann+1996]) and PoEAA [Fowler2002] (for information systems) (R3).

2.5.1 Explanation
In the following paragraphs you find explanations for the R1 patterns mentioned in LG 2-5. Some of the optional R3 patterns are briefly covered in the background section.

Layers
The term *layers* covers two different approaches:

- *Abstraction layers*: lower layers hide certain details from the layers above. Upper layers only access lower layers via clearly defined interfaces. The ISO/OSI network layers are a well-known example of this pattern. For details, see below in this section.
- Layers to *separate functionality* or responsibility. This approach is also known as *tiers*, like in "3-tier architecture". For example, a separation in presentation-, business- and data-access layers can be found in many information systems. Details are explained below in this section.

General observations

Some observations hold for all approaches to layering:

- Dependencies (e.g. function or method calls) go *down* from upper to lower layers only.
- Distinguish between *strict* and *loose* layering:
  - in a strict layer approach, communication from one layer is restricted to the layer immediately below it. Crossing layers is prohibited;
  - in loose layering, one layer may access all layers below it, dependencies or calls may bridge one or more intermediate layers.

See Figure 2.8 for an explanation.

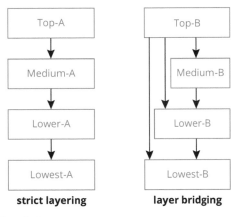

Figure 2.8 Strict layering versus layer-bridging

Advantages:

- Unidirectional dependencies between layers help to avoid circular dependencies;
- Simple structure, easy to understand.

Disadvantages:

- (Potentially) lower efficiency when requests from the uppermost layer cross several layer-boundaries until they reach the lower layers;
- (Potential) cascade of changes when the behavior of a single layer changes.

Abstraction layers

Abstraction layers hide certain details from the layer(s) above. Upper layers only access lower layers via clearly defined (public) interfaces.

Such a layer can exist without the layers above it, but *requires* the layers below it to function. The well-known and widely used ISO/OSI communication model consists of seven abstraction layers. Each layer of this model encapsulates and addresses a different part of digital communications.

In this specific case, *implementations* of those layers can be exchanged at runtime(!): When surfing the internet, you can switch between a cable-based to a wireless connection, without your internet browser (on layer 7) being aware of that change. However, runtime flexibility *can* be facilitated by layering, but this is not always the case.

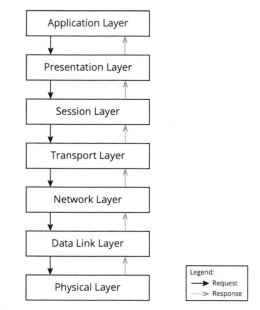

Figure 2.9 ISO/OSI Network Layers

These ISO/OSI network layers are defined as follows:
- Application Layer: High-level APIs, including remote file access;
- Presentation Layer: Translate data between networking service and application, including character encoding, data compression and encryption/decryption;
- Session Layer: Managing communication sessions, e.g. multiple back-and-forth transmissions between two nodes;
- Transport Layer: Reliable transmission of data segments, including acknowledgement;
- Network Layer: Structuring and managing a multi-node network, including addressing and routing;
- Data Link Layer: Reliable transmission of data frames between two nodes connected by a physical layer;
- Physical Layer: transmit and receive raw bit streams over a physical medium.

https://www.geeksforgeeks.org/layers-of-osi-model/ is a readable and comprehensive source explaining the ISO/OSI model in more detail.

The specific details of the ISO/OSI model are *not* required for the examination.

Functionality layers ("tiers")

A well-known architecture style, especially in information systems (e.g. Java-Enterprise Systems).

"Layered architecture focuses on the grouping of related functionality within an application into distinct layers that are stacked vertically on top of each other. Functionality within each layer is related by a common role or responsibility. Communication between layers is explicit and loosely coupled. Layering your application appropriately helps to support a strong separation of concerns that, in turn, supports flexibility and maintainability."

Quote from https://msdn.microsoft.com/en-us/library/ee658117.aspx#LayeredStyle

"Components within the layered architecture pattern are organized into horizontal layers, each layer performing a specific role within the application (e.g., presentation logic or business logic). Although the layered architecture pattern does not specify the number and types of layers that must exist in the pattern, most layered architectures consist of four standard layers: presentation, business, persistence, and database.

In some cases, the business layer and persistence layer are combined into a single business layer, particularly when the persistence logic (e.g., SQL or HSQL) is embedded within the business layer components. Thus, smaller applications may have only three layers, whereas larger and more complex business applications may contain five or more layers."

Quote from [Richards2015]

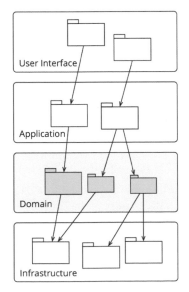

Figure 2.10 Functionality layers (tiers)

- Technical layers (like UI-layer, Service-layer) "hide" business- or domain-oriented structure;
- However, it potentially can be difficult to establish the correct granularity of functionality layers.

Pipes and filters

This pattern is an example of a *data flow* architecture: When processing a stream or batches of data, divide a (large) processing task into a sequence of smaller, independent processing steps (performed by *filters*) that are connected by channels (*pipes*).

Figure 2.11 Digital camera - a pipes and filters example

Filter: Transforms, aggregates or manipulates data. Receives input data from a pipe. A filter may have multiple input and/or output pipes.

Pipe: Transports data or messages between filters, without changing or altering them. A pipe may buffer data or messages until the receiving filter is able or willing to process that data.

Advantages:
- Simple (linear) dependencies;
- Flexible with regard to the processing steps involved;
- Allows for (relatively) simple scaling by executing filters in parallel (the corresponding pipes need to be enhanced to handle parallel filters, but the rest of the systems is not concerned);
- Pipes might remove the need for intermediate files;
- If the data stream has a standard format (like for example in Unix), filters can be developed independently.

Disadvantages:
- If a filter needs to wait until it has received *all* its input data (e.g. a sort filter), its incoming pipe (data buffer) might overflow;
- Errors might be difficult to track, as in the plain structure, no mechanism for error propagation exists (Unix instantiates a second pipe called `stdError` for this);
- It might (potentially) be difficult to share global or common data.

Microservices

The term "microservices" refers to an architectural style that divides larger systems into small, individually developable, deployable and operable units that communicate over networks.

Intent: Create highly flexible systems that can be adapted to changing user and business requirements as quickly as possible.

Problem: Monolithic applications often suffer from long development and turnaround cycles, as all of the various parts of the system have to be compiled, tested and deployed together. Especially in larger systems, that might lead to significant delays in the delivery of new features or fixes.

Solution: Create the overall system as a set of services that communicate via a network. Each service runs in its own process, and is deployable independent of other microservices. Data management of these services is mostly decentralized. Every microservice provides its own data storage, containing data to cover the required responsibilities.

Microservices combine existing concepts such as continuous delivery with new approaches to software architecture, system operation and team structure.

Advantages:
- Improve the changeability and flexibility of software.
- Improve time-to-market, i.e. new functions (features) as well as error corrections (fixes) can be brought into productive operation faster than before.
- Faster development by having smaller units, hence the name "microservices".
- Better capability for innovation and more flexibility in terms of technology selection - in principle, a development team responsible for one microservice can take their own technology decisions, (almost) independently of other microservice teams.
- Own runtime environment: Each microservice gets its own runtime environment. This adds to the independency, as microservices are supposed to communicate to each other only via network.
- Technology diversity (optional): Each microservice can be implemented in a technology best suited for the specific task.

Disadvantages:
- As microservices only communicate remotely, the typical $\rightarrow$ *fallacies of distributed computing* apply, including:
  - latency caused by (potentially slow) network connections;
  - outages of certain microservices or nodes due to network connection issues;
  - bandwidth limitations can disrupt communication.
- Due to these risks, additional precautions for error handling and recovery are required.
- Eventual consistency: Maintaining strong consistency is very difficult within distributed systems. Microservices most often deal with managing *eventual consistency*;
- Complexity shifts from architecture and implementation to deployment and operation of systems. You need a mature operations team to manage lots of services, which are being redeployed regularly. As microservices are developed (nearly) independently of each other, dependencies are resolved only at runtime (not at compile-time, as it is done with monolithic applications).
- Testing highly distributed microservices requires appropriate infrastructure.

These disadvantages sound dramatic upon first reading, but in recent years, several fundamental technologies have seen huge improvements:

- Networks, especially the Internet, have become increasingly stable, whilst bandwidth, throughput and capacity have increased;
- New generations of operating platforms have been created, for example container technology like Docker[22] and container management tools like Kubernetes[23].

Today, it's perfectly feasible to create highly distributed yet reliable systems.

Dependency injection

Intent: Defer dependency-resolution from compile-time to runtime. Developers don't need to decide which concrete or specific *detail* to use, but can create appropriate abstractions instead.

Problem: A component needs a service, but several variants, options or implementations of this service are available and you do not want to introduce dependencies for selection and creation into a component that needs a service.

Solution: Defer ("delay") the decision on which specific variant of the service to be used from compile time to runtime. Have a distinct component (called configurator, assembler, injector, builder or similar) create an appropriate service at runtime and *inject* this dependency into the component requiring this detail.

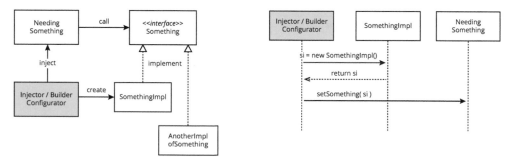

Figure 2.12 Static and dynamic model of dependency injection

In Figure 2.12, the "injector" creates an instance of a component implementing the "Something" interface and injects that instance into the "NeedingSomething" component. The injector needs to know which concrete variant to create, either by configuration, user-input or other means.

Dependency injection is not limited to object oriented systems: The main idea follows the →dependency inversion principle described in LG 2-6.

---

22 https://docker.com
23 https://kubernetes.io

Known applications:

- Under the generic term *Inversion of control* or *dependency inversion* or *Hollywood principle* ("Don't call us, we call you!") this pattern is used in frameworks of the Java enterprise world to reduce compile-time dependencies of components.
- The well-known Spring Framework https://spring.io is originally based upon the dependency injection pattern.
- In Java there's a standard approach called CDI (Contexts and Dependency Injection), included in Java Enterprise 6 and higher. It allows lifecycle management by injecting components (services) into client objects in flexible and type-safe way.

Advantages:

- Improved flexibility: As some decisions are deferred to runtime, you do not have to bother with the details of selecting and creating the specific component whose services are required.
- This unloads a lot of complexity that you typically would have to deal with from your component into the dependency injection framework you will normally use for this and also reduces coupling.
- If the real specific service is *expensive*, tests could be performed with *cheaper* mock instances.

Disadvantages:

- Due to the indirection and additional builder/injector/configurator component, code gets more complicated and might be more difficult to understand.
- The builder/injector/configurator is an additional source of errors.
- Some problems can only be detected at runtime, which would otherwise be detectable at compile time. Static analysis becomes hard, if not impossible, for some parts of your code.
- Misconfiguration can cause the whole system to break at runtime.

Further resources for patterns

POSA (Pattern Oriented Software Architecture) is a series of books on a variety of architecturally relevant patterns.

The series (currently) consists of the following volumes, published by Wiley. Wikipedia gives a compact overview[24] of these fundamental books:

- Volume 1: Frank Buschmann et al: Pattern-Oriented Software Architecture, A System of Patterns. Published 1996, contains e.g. layers, pipes and filters, blackboard, broker, MVC.
- Volume 2: Douglas Schmidt et al: Patterns for Concurrent and Networked Objects. Published 2000, very detailed coverage, with lots of C++ example code.
- Volume 3: Michael Kircher et al: Software Architecture Volume 3: Patterns for Resource Management. How to deal with limited resources like CPU or memory? Published 2004.
- Volume 4: Frank Buschmann et al: Pattern-Oriented Software Architecture Volume 4: A Pattern Language for Distributed Computing. Published 2007. Covers around 100 different patterns in very short format, excellent overview.

---

24 https://en.wikipedia.org/wiki/Pattern-Oriented_Software_Architecture

- Volume 5: Frank Buschmann et al: Pattern Oriented Software Architecture Volume 5: On Patterns and Pattern Languages. Published 2007.

 There are books and online resources available on several other architectural topics, like security, workflow-management, integration, requirements-analysis, stability and robustness, (business-)domain structure, releasing and operating systems, microservices and more. Although further patterns are not relevant for the examination, we very much urge aspiring architects to get an overview of *what is already available*, instead of trying to come up with self-made solutions. Patterns help to cure the *not-invented-here* syndrome.

2.5.2 Exercises

Discuss the arguments, both pro and contra, for layer bridging.

Consider at least maintainability, understandability, and runtime-performance aspects.

A-question: Which of the following properties are most likely to be improved by using the layer pattern?

Select the correct answer.

    [ ]   Runtime efficiency ("performance"),

    [x]   Flexibility for further development or changes to the system,

    [ ]   Flexibility at runtime ("configurability"),

    [ ]   Non-repudiability,

2.5.3 References

- Gregor Hohpe has given a short but concise explanation on pipes and filters:
  https://www.enterpriseintegrationpatterns.com/patterns/messaging/PipesAndFilters.html
- Chris Richardson [Richardson2018] has compiled a number of patterns for microservice architectures.
- Martin Fowler maintains an overview of resources on microservices,
  https://martinfowler.com/microservices/.
- LG 1-11 covers challenges of distributed computing, often encountered in microservice architectures.

LG 2-6: Design principles

Explain and use design principles (R1-R3)

Software architects are able to explain what design principles are. They can outline their general objectives and applications with regard to software architecture (R2).

Software architects are able to:
- Explain the design principles listed below and illustrate them with examples;
- Explain how those principles are to be applied;
- Explain how the requirements determine which principles should be applied;
- Explain the impact of design principles on the implementation;
- Analyze source code and architecture designs to evaluate whether these design principles have been applied or should be applied.

Abstraction (R1)
- In the sense of a means for deriving useful generalizations;
- As a design technique, where building blocks are dependent on the abstractions rather than depending on implementations;
- Interfaces as abstractions.

Modularization (R1-R3)
- Information hiding and encapsulation (R1);
- Separation of concerns - SoC (R1);
- Loose, but functionally sufficient, coupling (R1) of building blocks, see LG 2-7;
- High cohesion (R1);
- SOLID principles (R1-R3), which have, to a certain extent, relevance at the architectural level:
  - S: Single responsibility principle (R1) and its relation to SoC;
  - O: Open/closed principle (R1);
  - L: Liskov substitution principle (R3) as a way to achieve consistency and conceptual integrity in OO design;
  - I: Interface segregation principle (R2), including its relation to LG 2-9;
  - D: Dependency inversion principle (R1) by means of interfaces or similar abstractions.

Conceptual integrity (R2)
- Meaning uniformity (homogeneity, consistency) of solutions for similar problems (R2);
- As a means to achieve the principle of least surprise (R3).

Simplicity (R1-R2)
- As a means to reduce complexity (R1);
- As the driving factor behind KISS (R3) and YAGNI (R3).

Expect errors (R1-R2)
- As a means to design for robust and resilient systems (R1);
- As a generalization of the robustness principle (*Postel's law*) (R2).

Other principles (R3)
Software architects know other principles (such as CUPID, see [Nygard2022]), and can apply them.

2.6.1 Explanation

In LG 2-5 we described patterns that resemble "cooking recipes" for specific problems. What patterns essentially do is offer a proposal for the structured application of selected design principles to a specific problem. This learning goal introduces those general design principles and describes how they can be used to achieve architectural goals.

Abstraction and DRY

Abstraction is a crucial concept for handling complexity. It allows for having *not to deal* with all the details at once by omitting certain details.

In essence:
- Common features of a group of artifacts are separated into an abstraction of these artifacts.
- Details that make each artifact special and that have little or no ramifications outside its scope are left out.

Software architecture itself is an abstraction. It "omits certain information about elements that is not useful for reasoning about the system" [Bass+2021].

This principle may be applied in various ways:
- → *Interfaces* describe the public part of a component through which it interacts with its environment, while omitting private details about its implementation and internal structures. This allows you to *abstract* from those internal details when reasoning about constructing larger structures from these components and - within limits - to deal with components that provide the same abstraction in a similar manner.
- *Data abstractions* consider the abstract properties of data types while omitting details of their implementation.
- *Programming languages* are an abstraction from machine code. They enable you to declare your own abstractions, such as abstract functions, classes, data types, interfaces or lambdas.

Many more examples (e.g. layers or control abstraction) could be given, as abstraction is such a fundamental principle for reducing complexity and avoiding duplication.

The "Don't repeat yourself" or DRY principle heavily relies on the application of abstractions. B.C. Pierce phrased it from a programmer's perspective:

"Each significant piece of functionality in a program should be implemented in just one place in the source code. Where similar functions are carried out by distinct pieces of code, it is generally beneficial to combine them into one by abstracting out the varying parts."

Benjamin Crawford Pierce [Pierce2002]

This excellent advice for programmers applies to architects as well: Try to introduce abstractions for components that provide similar functionality. The DRY principle complements →*separation of concerns* and the →*single responsibility principle* quite well.

 Beware of abstractions that will only be used once, as they often make no sense. Bear in mind the principles of KISS and YAGNI (see the description of KISS later in this section).

Information hiding principle

The application of information hiding is so commonplace today that we use it almost subconsciously when writing software. When David Parnas described this principle back in 1972, software engineers had no systematic criteria for how to decompose software into distinct parts (formerly called modules, nowadays *building blocks*, components etc.).

"Information hiding" turned out to be one of the most fundamental and useful criterion for this task. By hiding design decisions within a module implementation, users of that module do not need to be aware of its inner workings. This allows developers to change such decisions easily, drastically reducing overall complexity.

 Actively hide the internals of a component. Users should be able to use it as a →black box without making assumptions about, for example, the specific algorithms or data structures used internally.

Separation of concerns

The idea behind SoC is to have different problems or tasks handled by different components, subsystems or layers of your architecture. The main focus is on deconstructing a problem into separate sub-problems or concerns, which is closely related to the single responsibility principle (see LG 2-6 on SRP).

For example, always separate business or domain-related concerns from the technical concerns of their implementation.

Consider a simple version of bank accounts: Their *business logic* (money is stored in and transferred between accounts) should be separated from the technical infrastructure required to store the balance of the account (database tables, files, objects, ...) and the means to manipulate them (database queries, transactions or specific function calls).

This separation should continue throughout the whole architecture. Transferring money between accounts is clearly different from creating account statements and should be handled by different building blocks. Collecting the data to be included in the account statement is handled separately from the process of formatting that statement into a printable document.

Besides separating concerns according to business- or domain functionality, common concerns that can be separated from another are e.g. persistence and presentation. Practically all of the patterns we have dealt with in LG 2-5 provide a "standardized" way of separating various concerns. For example, the pipes-and-filters patterns separate the flow of information between components ("pipes") from information processing or manipulation ("filters").

By keeping concerns separated you might end up with increased(!) coupling between components. This is a remarkable exception from the general rule to strive for loose coupling (see LG 2-6 on loose coupling). However, this is a fair price to pay as there is usually no way to get rid of the reasons that caused those components to be coupled in the first place. Separating concerns into different components helps to expose their relationship and dependencies more clearly.

Applying SoC assigns distinct responsibilities to the different parts of your system, which will increase changeability and analyzability.

 Always separate responsibilities so that you can describe each component's responsibility in a concise and short sentence.

Modularity

In general, *modularity* (also known as the building block principle) describes the division of a whole system into distinct building blocks (modules, building blocks, components etc.) with separate and defined responsibilities.

 Consistently applying SoC (separation of concerns) leads to modularity.

Modularity is a highly desirable quality attribute, as it combines the advantages of information hiding with SoC.

Modules have a number of desirable properties. They:
- Encapsulate responsibilities;
- Expose well defined interfaces only;
- Can be developed and maintained independently; and
- Can be replaced by other modules with identical interfaces without any side effects.

Therefore *modularity* enables several important architectural goals. Among others it ensures maintainability, comprehensibility, flexibility and testability.

Loose coupling

Components in a software system need to cooperate, therefore any component needs to have certain relations to other components. *Coupling* is the extent of such relationships. Higher coupling means more (mutual) relationships and a higher number of dependencies of any kind.

There is no way to get around *some* coupling, as components have to work together to provide a system's functionality. They call and use each other, create other components, rely on other components to be properly initialized before a functionality is available, or might require to be executed on the same machine to exchange data fast enough.

LG 2-7 will go into more details about the different ways or "modes" components can be coupled to each other.

When designing or changing a component, you need to consider the possible effects this change has on each of the coupled components. For example, after changing a data structure provided by one component, you have to make sure that all other components using this data structure still function properly. In addition you have to ensure that components are able to access this data structure only *after* it has been properly initialized.

 Coupling adds complexity: Coupling one component with another will make both components harder to understand and change. Highly coupled systems are more error-prone.

You *want* components to be loosely coupled. Those dependencies, which can't be eliminated, should be structured in a defined and explicit way.

 Couple components as loosely as possible without compromising functionality or missing quality goals.

The opposite of loose coupling are tightly coupled components, which often depend on details of each other's implementation. This might be necessary, for example, to meet performance requirements, but adds unwanted complexity. Overly tight coupling reduces analyzability, maintainability, flexibility and extensibility.

High cohesion

The *cohesion* of any component describes how closely the inner elements of this component are related to each other. Loose coupling and a well-done SoC usually correlate with high cohesion. It is an ordinal measurement, described as "low" or "high" and requires explicit criteria for evaluation. It *cannot be measured automatically* but can be quantified manually, for example by using a scoring board.

To illustrate bad cohesion with an example, imagine a system that applies the MVC pattern: In this do-not-do-this example *all* models are contained in a large package "models", all controllers end up in a package "controllers" and all views are put into the "views" package. This might be a very simple way to organize things, but those packages have a low cohesion as the views work more or less independently of each other. The models represent a wide variety of business aspects and the controllers are responsible for mostly unrelated behaviors.

It would be totally fine to decompose *a single business component* into those three sub-packages. Its models, views and controllers would certainly interact closely with each other. However, it is a bad idea to have such large system-wide packages as this leads to the undesirable consequence that they are difficult to understand, modify, test and reuse.

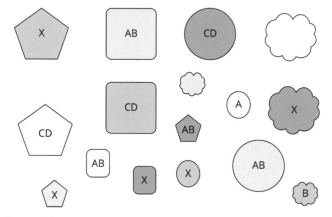

Figure 2.13 Unordered group of elements

Cohesion combines those elements that (for some criterion!) belong together. Consider the example of an unordered group (shown in Figure 2.13) of *elements* of different shape, size, color and text. How can we combine those elements into *cohesive* modules? Obviously there are a number of different ways of achieving this.

Figure 2.14 gives three examples for a valid grouping/ordering of these elements:

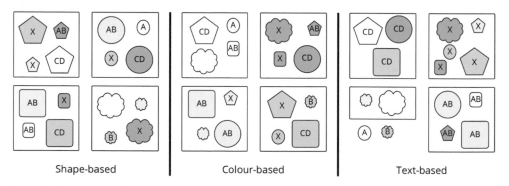

Shape-based   Colour-based   Text-based

Figure 2.14 Elements, grouped by various criteria

 Strive for high cohesion to limit the impact of changes to a small cluster of components and to place closely related functionality into closely related components.

SOLID (R1-R3)

Many developers are familiar with the SOLID principles[25] used in object-oriented design.

The acronym SOLID stands for:
- Single responsibility principle;
- Open–closed principle;
- Liskov substitution principle;
- Interface segregation principle;
- Dependency inversion principle.

As the scope of software architecture extends beyond object-oriented systems and we like to avoid discussing highly specific programming rules, the following sections are going to bridge a gap.

We will focus on the *concepts* behind the SOLID principles applicable on an architectural level ("in-the-large").

Single responsibility principle (R1)

The single-responsibility principle (SRP) pursues the same objectives as SoC (separation of concerns), though from a different perspective.

While the SRP states that a component should be responsible for a single concern, SoC is about dividing a system into components in such a way that their concerns overlap as little as possible.

A component should:
- Be responsible for *only one* clearly defined functionality of the system;
- Contain only functions or sub-components directly contributing to this functionality;
- Encapsulate this functionality;
- Have only "one reason to change[26]".

For a monolithic report generator, as depicted in Figure 2.15, several reasons to change do exist, e.g. when reports need to contain different items or when they should be printed in another layout. A modular report generator component changes when further components with additional sub-functionalities are included. Its sub-components will change only for very specific singular reasons.

---

25 https://en.wikipedia.org/wiki/SOLID
26 https://blog.cleancoder.com/uncle-bob/2014/05/08/SingleReponsibilityPrinciple.html

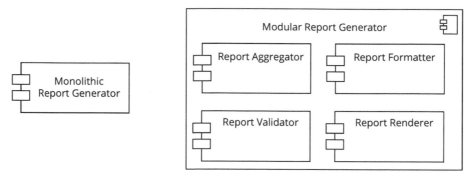

Figure 2.15 Monolithic vs. modular report generator as an example for SoC and the SRP

Open-closed principle (R1)

It is reasonable to expect that certain parts of your software system will be extended to include features that are currently not fully specified or that the customer does not yet want to pay for. Likewise, it can be assumed that certain technologies, e.g. logging or persistence frameworks, will be replaced by more modern solutions in the foreseeable future. This makes "flexibility" and "extensibility" an important architectural requirement.

However, such changes should be possible with minimal modifications to existing components and should have as few side effects as possible to avoid extensive, expensive and risky re-design or re-implementation efforts. You can avoid them by adhering to the open-closed principle:

> Components should be open for extension, but closed for modification. You want to be able to *extend* their functionality without modifying the component itself.

Achieving this property can actually be quite simple, as several options exist:
- Inheritance in object-oriented systems;
- Plug-in architectures (see LG 2-5 on patterns);
- The dependency inversion principle or the use of dependency injection frameworks.

Liskov substitution principle

The Liskov substitution principle (LSP) is a way to promote consistency and conceptual integrity, but refers to object-oriented systems. The concept behind it, however, applies to architectural design in general, as it tries to avoid unexpected behavior or inconsistencies in the use of components.

In the OO-way, the LSP requires that an instance of subclass can be used in the same way as an instance of the superclass - with no strings attached. You should not need to worry about possibly changed semantics of methods, side effects, or additional needs for initialization and clean-up operations (e.g. closing file handles). This more general interpretation helps you with designing specializations and abstractions. You should strive for implementations that can be used as drop-in-replacements for their abstractions.

Interface segregation principle

The interface segregation principle (ISP) is just one of many guidelines that are relevant for the design of interfaces. In case you require more background on the ISP, please refer to LG 2-9, which deals exclusively with the design and definition of interfaces.

 Smaller and client-specific interfaces might lead to lower coupling and fewer dependencies than large "universal" or "generic" interfaces.

Dependency inversion principle (R1)

Designing and structuring dependencies belongs to one of the most important aspects of software architecture design.

When a component depends upon certain details (e.g. a path to a configuration file), and this detail changes (e.g. the configuration file is moved to a new location), the component will likely cease working.

The dependency inversion principle (DIP) advises *not* to depend on low-level details, but rather to depend on abstractions. Components should be decoupled from changes in details by using abstractions (e.g. interfaces) instead. As long as these abstractions remain stable, everything is fine.

There are several ways to achieve this decoupling:
- More often than not, components that *implement* functionality also provide the →interface to use it. This interface is often an inherent part of the module you use. It might not even provide an abstraction, but perhaps only consists of the signature of a particular function in your implementation. Such an **Application Programming Interface (API)** is called a **provided interface**. A high-level component that uses functionality frequently depends on an interface defined by a low-level component. However, if something changes in the lower layers of your system, you may need to modify high-level components, which is not desirable at all.
- There is a way around this: Let components *using* a functionality define the interface to use it (called **Service Programming Interface (SPI)** or **required interface**). In this case the component that implements a functionality needs to adhere to this already defined interface. The dependency is now **inverted**.

 High-level modules should not depend on low-level modules. Both should depend on abstractions (e.g. interfaces). Abstractions should not depend on details. Specializations (e.g. specific implementations) should depend on abstractions.

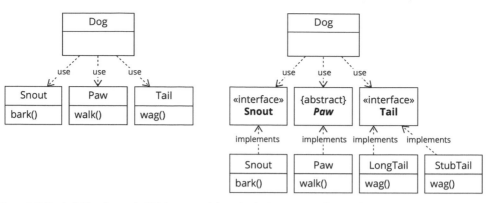

Figure 2.16 Poorly (left) and properly (right) structured dependencies in a canine application domain

Conceptual integrity

Try to strive for → conceptual integrity and consistency. The entire design of your system should follow a consistent style. Similar tasks should be handled in a similar manner.

Avoid components that behave in wildly unexpected ways, have unexpected prerequisites or are structured according to some arcane criteria. Sometimes called the *Principle of least astonishment* (or least surprise), this helps to facilitate understanding and further development of a system.

When designing a new component or feature, think about how things are handled in existing parts of your software system and how a programmer or another architect would expect them to work. Try to develop a consistent "design philosophy" or "style" like:

- Unix: Everything is a file;
- SQL: Everything resides in tables (yes, even most configuration data);
- Lisp: Everything is a list.

> *"Conceptual integrity is the most important consideration in system design. It is better to have a system omit certain anomalous features and improvements, but to reflect one set of design ideas, than to have one that contains many good but independent and uncoordinated ideas."*

Frederick P. Brooks [Brooks1975]

Keep things simple - KISS and YAGNI

The principles "Keep it small and simple" (KISS) and "You ain't gonna need it" (YAGNI) are helpful guidelines for discussing design alternatives.

Some members of the IT workforce tend to over-engineer on certain problems in order to provide solutions that can handle *all imaginable* future extensions and corner cases:

- Abstractions are forced onto components where just a single implementation exists, that is used in just one place by only one other component.
- Functionality is added that eventually might become useful in the future.
- Complicated or high-sophisticated technology is used, where a very simple approach would suffice.

All in the hope of saving on future development efforts, which in most cases never come. Instead, KISS proposes to:

- Design the simplest thing that does the job for the foreseeable future without overly constraining your design space.
- Provide abstractions in a sensible way. That is, for those components that actually require flexibility and extensibility or are used by a significant number of other components.
- Trust future architects to be able to derive a more sophisticated solution if the need should arise.

Simplicity helps to keep systems understandable (and therefore changeable) over time - enabling and facilitating future changes.

Expect errors

"What can possibly go wrong?" is a question that should not be dismissed lightly in systems design. At the end of the day, it's not the errors you were expecting that make your life difficult, but the things you have turned your back on:

- Always be on the lookout for things that can go wrong.
- Ask yourself what other people might misunderstand, forget or neglect.
- Which parts of a software system can fail and what are the implications?

If resilience, stability, reliability and availability of a system are important, consider Murphy's Law in its original wording: "If there's more than one possible outcome of a job or task, and one of those outcomes will result in disaster or an undesirable consequence, then somebody will do it that way."

The *robustness principle*, also known as Postel's Law can be helpful when designing mission critical systems. It recommends that you should "Be conservative in what you do, be liberal in what you accept from others." That is, design a component in such a way that it will still work even if it is not used correctly. Try to use other components as correctly as possible and according to their specifications. This will make your system more fault-tolerant, and it may still be able to maintain functionality even if parts of it fail. This capability is known as *graceful degradation*.

However, this comes at a price:

- Additional complexity is required to compensate for errors, which leads to a larger system size and may introduce potential secondary errors.
- Data exchanged via interfaces may no longer be correct.
- Others might take advantage of very tolerant components and neglect being strict at their outgoing interfaces, resulting in reduced consistency and integrity of the software system.

2.6.2 Exercises

A-question: What is the objective of the dependency inversion principle?

Select the correct answer.

[ ]   Large components should not depend on small components.

[ ]   Components should be able to create dependent components more easily.

[x]   If possible, components should only depend on each other via interfaces.

P-question: Which statements about the principle "Don't repeat yourself" are correct?

Select the two most appropriate.

[ ]   Strict adherence to DRY could lead to poor modularization.

[x]   Strict adherence to DRY can lead to tighter coupling between modules.

[x]   The components, which previously contained redundant parts, can now be more
        easily modified and extended independently of each other.

[ ]   Compliance with DRY usually increases attack vectors in IT security.

[ ]   Only the application of the dependency inversion principle enables a consistent
        application of the DRY principle.

[ ]   The application of the DRY principle reduces the re-usability of components.

LG 2-7: Managing dependencies

Managing dependencies between building blocks (R1)

Software architects understand dependencies and coupling between building blocks and can use them in a targeted manner. They:

- Know and understand different types of dependencies of building blocks (e.g. coupling via use/delegation, messaging/events, composition, creation, inheritance, temporal coupling, coupling via data, data types or hardware);
- Understand how dependencies increase coupling;
- Can use such types of coupling in a targeted manner and can assess the consequences of such dependencies;
- Know and can apply possibilities to reduce or eliminate coupling, for example:
  - patterns, see LG 2-5;
  - basic design principles, see LG 2-6;
  - externalization of dependencies, i.e. defining concrete dependencies at installation or runtime, for example by using dependency injection.

2.7.1 Explanation

Dependency

A component Comp *depends* on component Req if it requires or needs Req, for example to:

- Compile (compile-time dependency);
- Be installed;
- Be tested;
- Start (e.g. Req is needed to create and/or configure Comp or contains data that Comp requires);
- Run or function properly.

In these cases Comp is called a *dependent* component which has a *dependency* to Req.

Coupling

The degree of dependence between arbitrary elements (like components, building-blocks, functions, etc.). Coupling is a measure of how closely two elements depend on each other. Some coupling is necessary when creating software, for example to delegate responsibilities between different modules. Note that coupling might be directional.

Risks and problems

Risks and problems caused by dependencies and coupling include at least the following:

- Changing one component may require changes in other components (*ripple effect*);
- Compiling, building and testing components might require additional effort due to dependencies;
- A component might be harder to reuse and/or test because components it depends on need to be included;
- Understanding a component becomes more difficult, as one potentially has to understand the components it depends on or sometimes even the dependent components.

Types of coupling

Several different types (or categories) of coupling exist - we will briefly cover a few of those. As often within the curriculum, please note the exemplary nature of the enumeration within this LG: The iSAQB does not regard this enumeration as complete and there are some more sophisticated and fine grained approaches to classify coupling - consequently it is out-of-scope for this book to provide a *complete* treatment of this topic.

Therefore, let's concentrate on several typical and widespread types of coupling.

> **!** It's important to note that different types or categories of coupling exist. Some (but not all) types of coupling can be identified by analyzing the source code of an IT system.

Coupling via use/delegation

A *usage* or *delegation* is a method or function call that originates in one component and is handled by another.

Within delegations, the following two variants are possible as depicted in the diagram:

1. (Very bad): Component **X** uses some internal detail of component **Y**. If these details of **Y** are ever modified, then **X** is likely to break. This kind of design or programming should be avoided, as it is sensitive to even small changes (*brittle*).
2. (Better): Component **C** uses a public interface of component **Req.** **C** neither needs to know about the internal structure of **Req**, nor about internal data types or algorithms. **Req** is used as a black box. As long as the public interface remains stable, the internals of **Req** can be changed, giving this kind of dependency at least some degree of flexibility.

In programming languages with a good modularization concept, the first (very bad) variant can be avoided on a language level, e.g. by declaring certain internal parts as `private`.

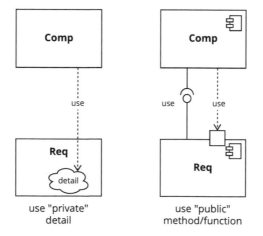

Figure 2.17 Variants of use/delegation

Coupling via composition

In composition relationships, one component contains another, for example "car contains engine". The containing component is coupled to the contained component(s) or component types. In some cases, the contained component (the *part*) cannot exist without the containing component (the *whole*), e.g. "human contains brain", where the brain cannot exist without its containing human.

> **!** The finer distinction between aggregation and composition from an object-oriented design or
> **●** UML perspective is not relevant for the examination.

Coupling via creation

If one component (`Factory`) is needed to create (instances of) component `Comp`, then `Comp` is coupled to `Factory`.

From the object-oriented design patterns you might remember the creational patterns, like AbstractFactory. They provide a uniform way of handling coupling via creation and therefore improve → consistency.

Coupling via inheritance

A relationship where a subclass inherits properties and methods either from:

* A superclass (class-based inheritance like in Java, C++ or C#). Some languages (e.g. C++) even allow for multiple inheritances, so that a subclass can have multiple different superclasses. Subclasses inherit the implementation (the code) of methods implemented in the superclass(es).
* An interface, so that the subclass does not inherit concrete implementation, just the signature.
* Another instance or object (prototype-based inheritance, like in JavaScript).

In a more general perspective, components (*children*) inherit properties from other components (*parents*). The coupling via inheritance is very tight, as the child carries all the burden (*ballast*) of their parents.

Coupling via interface-inheritance is lower, as the interface defines only what the subclass has to implement, but does not burden the subclass with concrete implementation(s).

Coupling via messages or events

Various definitions exist for messages and events - but with some commonalities:

Message: A request from one component (`sender`) to another for an action to be taken Messages might be sent to a specific recipient or made available to any component. A `sender` may or may not know what component(s) are receiving and processing the message. Usually, the `sender` expects the message to be processed somehow, but does not expect a reply (asynchronous communication).

Event: A message which informs various arbitrary listeners about something which has happened. Events are sent by a producer that does not know which other components receive the event.

! Subtle distinctions between messages and events are not part of the examination, as such differ-
● ences are often technology- or product-specific.

Components communicating by events or messages are loosely coupled because producers:
- Do not know which consumers are listening for their messages or event;
- Do not know about the consequences of messages or events;
- Do not expect a synchronous reply, so there is no temporal coupling (see below).

Temporal coupling

Temporal coupling belongs to the (many) terms in software engineering that are overloaded with several, slightly different, meanings. Various authors came up with different definitions - all with their own nuances. Please see the Glossary for details.

The common ground of these definitions is the following:
- Temporal coupling is an (implicit) relationship between two or more components in the temporal dimension.

Let's try a more concrete version: If a component `Comp` can only perform a task if another component `Req` has completed another task - then `Comp` temporarily depends on `Req`.

A simple example of temporal coupling can be seen in online banking applications. Users have to authenticate with their (secret) credentials before they can perform any actual banking transactions. The core banking component(s) temporarily depend on the authentication component.

Such temporal coupling does not require the coupled components to share code, be written in the same language or even know about each other, the prerequisite of the temporal order of processing, tasks or functions might be the only dependency between `Comp` and `Req`.

Temporal coupling will often occur together with *shared state* or *global state*.

Coupling via data types

If one component `Comp` uses a specific data type declared or defined in or by another component `Req`, then this is obviously a dependency. This is a very common case in programming - defining data types in one component and having other components use the same type. It creates coupling between the components *using* the type definition.

Consider the situation from the following diagram: If component 'CompA' requires a modification of the type defined in `SpecialDataType`, then all other components `CompB`, `CompC` etc. need to consider this update too!

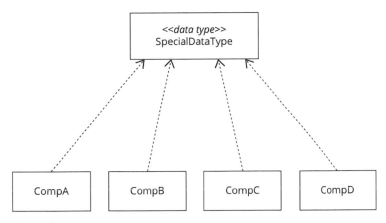

Figure 2.18 Coupling via data type

The subtle difference between *declaration* and *definition* of data types is not part of the curriculum or examination.

Coupling via data

Imagine a component `Comp` that receives data from a database, a configuration file or an environment variable. That data determines or configures the behavior of Comp, therefore it is crucial. Imagine a second component, `Req`, which creates or manipulates that data (see Figure 2.19).

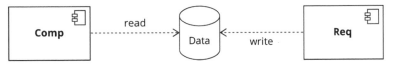

Figure 2.19 Coupling via data

With respect to source code, `Comp` and `Req` can be completely different programs, systems or components. Their commonality is the (shared) data, in the diagram depicted as a database, but it can be a file or environment variable too.

Although `Comp` has no direct dependency towards `Req`, these two are coupled over the (shared) data.

Please note that the component manipulating ("writing") such data need not be aware that another component is using this data. `Req` might consider the data private and does not know about `Comp`. When something in `Comp` fails due to changes in such data, debugging can become very difficult.

Coupling via hardware

Consider the following examples for coupling based upon hardware:

- Two processes exist in the same physical hardware, one of them reads specific memory locations that the other has written (see diagram below).
- A component is encrypted and can only run on hardware that has the appropriate encryption key baked into a specific memory location.

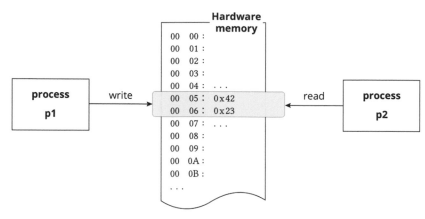

Figure 2.20 Coupling via hardware

Coupling via hardware might occur when doing low-level programming, like using system calls that depend on specific hardware. An example is programming for vendor-specific GPUs (graphical processing units), e.g. CUDA[27], which can be used to speed up parallel algorithms.

Dependencies and coupling

Coupling creates dependencies, therefore dependencies are a consequence of coupling. You can use the terms interchangeably.

Some dependencies are required to make components, modules or other architectural building blocks collaborate.

Options to reduce coupling

As we encounter different types or categories of coupling, we need different approaches to handle them.

Some examples:
* Use- or call-dependencies between two components could be removed by relocating the called or used method/function into the caller, e.g. by a move-method or move-function refactoring.
* Apply the dependency-inversion principle, and for example, replace a direct call with a call to an interface.
* Use patterns like broker or → registry to replace direct and tight coupling between components.
* Replace synchronous communication (usually involving temporal coupling) by asynchronous communication via events or messages.
* Introduce redundancy: For example you could replace a shared database by several, component-specific datastores with appropriate collaboration mechanisms. That's what strategic design in domain-driven design and microservices often proposes.

---

27 https://developer.nvidia.com/about-cuda

! Different types or categories of dependencies can exist between elements of a system. Only some of these (but not all) can be found by analyzing the system's source code.

2.7.2 Exercises

K-question: What are indicators for tight (high) or loose (low) coupling?

Select the correct choice for each answer option.

tight coupling	loose coupling	
[x]	[ ]	Building blocks call their dependent building blocks directly instead of calling them via interfaces or abstractions.
[x]	[ ]	Building blocks rely on the use of some shared data types.
[x]	[ ]	Building blocks use the same database.
[ ]	[x]	The implementation of building blocks consistently adheres to the dependency inversion principle.

Reflect on potential disadvantages of coupling or dependencies

Think about the following aspects with respect to coupling or dependencies:
- Technical (e.g. a component requiring a certain framework or library to run);
- Organizational (e.g. what consequences can technical dependencies have on development teams and their structure?);
- Deployment/rollout (e.g. what can happen in deployment/rollout if certain components depend on each other?).

Reflect on what kind of coupling can be identified in source code

Often a simple call-relationship will be explicitly written in source code. Think of coupling that can *not* be found when analyzing the source code of the corresponding component - and think of options or approaches to find such dependencies.

Reflect on additional options to reduce coupling

Apart from the few examples provided above, what other approaches, patterns, tactics or strategies can you imagine that could help reduce coupling? What are the potential side-effects (*disadvantages*) of these approaches?

2.7.3 References

Astonishingly, there is no established consensus of *categories (or types, or modes) of coupling* in the software engineering community.

In case you want to read more about the subject, the Wikipedia article https://en.wikipedia.org/wiki/Coupling_(computer_programming) on coupling can be a start.

A recent academic meta-study by Fregnan et al. [Fregnan+2019] explains more than 20 different categories. From our personal perspective, such a fine-grained but highly overlapping schema might provide interesting insights but is only of limited value in day-to-day architectural decisions.

LG 2-8: Achieve quality requirements

Achieve quality requirements with appropriate approaches and techniques (R1)

Software architects understand and consider the considerable influence of quality requirements in making architecture and design decisions, e.g. for:

- Efficiency, runtime performance;
- Availability;
- Maintainability, modifiability, extensibility, adaptability;
- Energy efficiency.

They can:

- Explain and apply solution options, *architectural tactics*, suitable practices as well as technical possibilities to achieve important quality requirements of software systems (different for embedded systems or information systems);
- Identify and communicate possible trade-offs between such solutions and their associated risks.

2.8.1 Explanation

In the day-to-day work of software architects, this will likely be one of the most important goals, as quality requirements are often considerably difficult to achieve!

You should know the quality requirements of your most important stakeholders, since they will often fundamentally influence architectural decisions. Make sure to be very on-point, specific and expressive about these qualities, avoiding any buzzwords.

Quality scenarios (see LG 4-2) are a simple and established method to make quality requirements explicit.

Be aware of interdependencies and trade-offs between such qualities: For example, great runtime performance (*good!*) often achieved by caching, parallel execution, sophisticated pre-loading strategies and such, quite often increases code size and complexity (*bad!*). For additional information on trade-offs see LG 2-2.

Architectural tactics to achieve quality requirements

The term → *architectural tactics* has been coined by Len Bass and his colleagues from the Software Engineering Institute (SEI) and is extensively described in [Bass+2021].

Such an architectural tactic is any action, approach, tactic, strategy, plan, procedure or similar with the intention to achieve a certain quality requirement.

The following sections contain only brief descriptions of such tactics for some selected quality attributes.

Performance tactics

To systematically achieve performance requirements, you can distinguish at least the following categories:

- Manage *resource demand*, e.g. by reducing computational overhead, exerting bounds on execution times, increasing efficiency of algorithms.
- Manage *resources*, e.g. by balancing resource allocation, increasing resources, maintaining multiple copies of data or computation nodes.
- *Arbitrate between conflicting demands*, e.g. by implementing appropriate scheduling policies, using synchronization protocols or increasing the level of concurrency.

Availability tactics

To systematically achieve availability requirements, you can distinguish at least the following categories:

- Detect faults, e.g. by using ping, heartbeat, sanity checking, monitoring, voting, self-tests or detecting exceptions.
- Recover from faults, e.g. by using redundancy, exception handing, rollbacks, retries, or ignoring faulty behavior.
- Prevent faults, e.g. by removing parts of the system from active service, using transactions, or preventing exceptions.

Maintainability or modifiability tactics

To systematically achieve modifiability or maintainability requirements, you can distinguish at least the following categories:

- Localize expected changes, e.g. by reducing the size of modules, splitting modules, encapsulating, reducing dependencies and coupling, using intermediaries, or isolating expected changes.
- Restrict visibility of responsibilities, e.g. hiding information, keeping interfaces constant across changes, separating interfaces from implementation.
- Avoid ripple effects, e.g. by breaking dependency chains, making data self-identifying, limiting communication paths.

2.8.2 Exercises

Reflect on possible tactics or approaches to achieve quality requirements, especially:

- testability;
- security;
- usability.

P-question: ISO 25010 provides generic quality characteristics for software systems. How can quality requirements concerning these characteristics be made more concrete? Pick the *two* best alternatives.

      [ ]   By developing UI prototypes.

      [x]   By discussing or writing quality scenarios.

      [ ]   By defining explicit interfaces.

      [x]   By creating a quality tree.

      [ ]   By creating automatic tests.

2.8.3 References

- LG 4-2 introduces quality requirements, the prerequisite for achieving quality.
- LG 2-2 explains trade-offs between conflicting quality requirements.
- [Bass+2021] introduces the term "architectural tactics" for generic approaches to achieving certain quality attributes.

LG 2-9: Design and define interfaces

Design and define interfaces (R1-R3)

Software architects know about the importance of interfaces. They are able to design or specify interfaces between architectural building blocks as well as external interfaces between the system and elements outside of the system.

They know:
- Desired characteristics of interfaces and can use them in the design:
  - easy to learn, easy to use, easy to extend;
  - hard to misuse;
  - functionally complete from the perspective of users or building blocks using them;
- The necessity to treat internal and external interfaces differently;
- Different approaches for implementing interfaces (R3):
  - resource oriented approach (REST, Representational State Transfer);
  - service oriented approach (see WS-*/SOAP-based web services).

2.9.1 Explanation

Interfaces define and describe the collaboration between different architectural elements.

You can distinguish between different interface *categories*:
- *Provided* interfaces or *Application Programming Interfaces* (API): These abstract from an underlying implementation and expose only what is needed to *use* the provided functions or data.
- *Service Provider Interface* (SPI) is an API intended to be implemented or extended by another component or system. It can be used to enable extensions to a given component or system.
- *Required* interfaces describe what a component *needs* in order to fulfill its responsibilities.

A *consumer* (sometimes called a client) is a component using the interface to invoke a functionality (service, process) or get data from a service *provider*.

What belongs to an interface?

The following aspects can be important for the design and implementation of interfaces:
- Syntax, e.g. names and types used, method- or function names available in the interface.
- Semantic, the meaning or responsibilities of interface elements.
- Protocol, the detailed interactions between consumer and provider, including required order of calls/events, prerequisites, pre- and/or post-conditions.
- Physical or technical media used for the interaction. Consumer and provider *might* reside in the same address space within a single computer, or on different runtime environments.
- In such a simple case, physical transport is not an issue. In the case of remotely distributed consumer and provider, the characteristics of the physical transport (*network*) will surely influence the interface.
- Required *quality* characteristics, like performance efficiency, load, throughput, reliability.

- Such requirements will influence both the interface and its implementation.
- *Versioning* and compatibility requirements: does the interface need versioning or backward compatibility?

Requirements on interfaces and best practices

The following aspects can be important for the design and implementation of interfaces:

- Interfaces should fit the needs of the components that use them and convey an adequate access to the functionality that is provided (or to be implemented in the case of required interfaces or SPIs).
- Therefore clarify requirements with the consumer and the provider.
- They should be easy to learn and easy to use. Consider providing, for example, unit tests as an addition to their documentation to show how it's done.
- When designing an interface, try to use it yourself, implement tests, and use those tests as a reference example.
- In doing so, you will find out how the interface "feels" for consumers or extended service providers.
- Provide "atomic" information units that are easy to evaluate, e.g. without complex parsing of returned strings.
- When your client code that consumes an interface starts to get complicated there is a high probability that something is wrong with the interface design.
- Design with extensibility in mind when requirements are likely to change. More often than not they will.
- Introducing API versioning right from the start can be helpful.
- Build things in way that makes them hard to misuse (intentional and unintentional).
- Hide implementation details (see → information hiding principle).
- Be consistent with other interfaces in the system. Use similar naming schemes, conventions, and concepts.
- Use meaningful, self-descriptive names, e.g. terms from the domain model.
- Minimize surprises and side effects. Whenever there are edge cases, provide ample documentation.

2.9.2 Exercises

K-question: What are guidelines for good interface design? Check which of the following statements are true and which are false.

True	False	
[x]	[ ]	Use of interfaces should be easy to learn.
[ ]	[x]	Interfaces specifications need to be understood by all stakeholders, and therefore should be written in natural language.
[ ]	[x]	An interface should be defined by the provider of the appropriate service.
[x]	[ ]	The client code should be easy to understand.
[x]	[ ]	Interfaces specifications should contain functional and non-functional aspects.

2.9.3 References

Concepts related to *interfaces* are covered in several learning goals:

- Dependency inversion in LG 2-6;
- Describing interfaces in LG 3-7.

[Geewax2020] describes good practices regarding (web) APIs, based upon experience at Google.

LG 2-10: Principles of software deployment

Know Fundamental Principles of Software Deployment (R3)

Software architects:

- Know that software deployment is the process of making new or updated software available to its users;
- Are able to name and explain fundamental concepts of software deployment, for example:
  - automated deployments;
  - repeatable builds;
  - consistent environments (e.g. use immutable and disposable infrastructure);
  - put everything under version-control;
  - releases are easy-to-undo.

2.10.1 Explanation

! This learning goal is not relevant for the examination.

Some readers may remember the days when your new operating system arrived as a bunch of floppy disks in a cardboard box. Things have changed significantly since then.

While some organizations still make new or updated software available through a manual deployment on the customer's hardware, others have opted for a highly automated approach. Among other reasons, this is because the growing adoption of distributed architectures results in more fine-grained deployment models, while monoliths usually deliver a single deployable artifact.

What to consider?

"Making software available" sounds like the easy part after all the hard work is done. But consider demanding availability and reliability requirements, where downtimes for fixing errors that made their way into production will cost you dearly. There's a reason why "Don't deploy on Friday!" is a popular mantra among "older" developers.

Good practices for deployment start with a well-defined process that is coordinated with relevant stakeholders (e.g. users, operations, testers) who need to be ready for changes or are actively involved. Consider that things could go wrong. Therefore, a contingency plan for a rollback should be established in advance.

Even if you don't use continuous delivery, deployment involves more than simply copying software to the production environment. Often, the required runtime environment must also be provided and configured. Consider the following potential issues which might have to be addressed before or during deployments:

- Operating system setup and configuration, ensuring the required versions or patch levels are in place.

- Set user and respective access rights for the target file system.
- Set network and firewall configuration, including the configuration of VPNs.
- Setup of cryptographic certificates.
- Database setup, with tablespaces, schema, indices, users, and respective access rights.
- Provide eventually required data or database migrations.
- Pre-loading databases with required data.
- Ensuring that required configuration files are present and accessible.
- Make sure, required external libraries or frameworks are available in correct locations.

Investing in a high level of automation can therefore be worthwhile and help to reduce the risk of human error. Extensive testing in a staging environment can reduce the likelihood of errors creeping into production systems. By monitoring the deployment process, product performance and the state of the environment, you can respond more quickly to those that have slipped through anyway.

Deployment strategies
Different deployment strategies offer different trade-offs between simplicity, speed, cost, and risks that impact, e.g., availability and performance.
- Basic deployment (recreate deployment): The old version of the application is stopped and replaced by the new version.
- Rolling deployment (ramped deployment): This is only applicable when multiple instances of an application serve user requests. Here, old instances are gradually replaced with new versions.
- Blue/green deployment: The old (blue) and new (green) version of the application are deployed simultaneously. After testing the new version, users are redirected to it.
- Shadow deployment: While being quite similar to blue/green deployment, user requests are forked and sent to both versions while users only receive responses from the old version.
- Canary deployment: Initially only a small fraction of users is served by the new version in order to check for any problems. This fraction is gradually increased until the old version is completely replaced. This strategy can also be used to get user feedback on new features (A/B-testing).

2.10.2 Exercises
Consider the impact of different deployment strategies on design and development cycles. What implications do they have for the availability and maintainability of an IT system? Try to identify trade-offs regarding initial and ongoing development effort, complexity, resource usage, and time-to-market. Could highly distributed systems even be built and maintained efficiently without at least some degree of automatization for deployment?

2.10.3 References
A quick introduction to software deployment strategies and a deployment checklist is provided by https://codefresh.io/learn/software-deployment/.

Substantial parts of [Nygard2018] cover the topic with emphasis on designing for deployment and deployments without downtime.

CPSA-F Chapter 3: Specification and communication of software architectures

LG 3-1: Requirements of technical documentation

Explain and consider the requirements of technical documentation (R1)

Software architects know the requirements of technical documentation and can consider and fulfil them when documenting systems:

- Understandability, correctness, efficiency, appropriateness and maintainability;
- Form, content and level of detail tailored to the stakeholders.

They know that only the target audiences can assess the understandability of technical documentation.

3.1.1 Explanation

When creating and maintaining technical documentation you need to satisfy several fundamental requirements. Some of those might seem obvious, but are very often neglected in reality.

Documentation requirement 1: Correct

Incorrect information in (technical) documentation can be as bad as software bugs. Even worse, readers who find mistakes in one part of the documentation quickly lose their trust in the rest. The perceived value of the documentation vastly decreases.

Therefore, one important requirement for documentation is its correctness. Never (ever!) allow incorrect information in documentation. Correctness is the highest goal that you should never jeopardize!

Documentation requirement 2: Current

Correctness of documentation changes over time. What was correct yesterday could already be wrong today. You want your documentation to be current.

Documentation requirement 3: Helpful

Documentation has to help all readers to perform their concrete tasks. It should ease or facilitate their work. Therefore the following relation must be true:

$$\text{Effort}_{\text{with documentation}} < \text{Effort}_{\text{without documentation}}$$

Even during system development architecture documentation should be helpful and not regarded as an unnecessary burden requiring extra effort.

Documentation requirement 4: Easy to change

Every change (enhancements, reconstructions, maintenance, and even bug fixes) to your system can lead to necessary changes in the documentation. The easier it is for developers to keep documentation current, the higher the chances that the documentation actually gets updated.

On the other hand, if changing the documentation is difficult and costly, it is simply not done. Documentation will then quickly become outdated, losing its correctness.

Documentation requirement 5: Easy to understand

Consumers (readers) have to easily understand the documentation. Documentation has to fulfill their expectations in several dimensions: language, notation, form and tooling.

Easier said than done - because sometimes the producers of documentation do not (yet) know all of the consumers who might need that documentation in the future.

As an author of documentation, you should definitely invest adequate effort to ensure understandability, e.g., through reviews and incorporating reader feedback.

Documentation requirement 6: Easy to find

Consumers shall be able to find information easily and quickly within the documentation. Fixed structures or templates (like → arc42) and conventions help with that. See LG 3-2.

Documentation requirement 7: Adequate

Frankly, we don't know how much documentation you really need for your system, how detailed you need it, and which notation your readers are comfortable with. The *stakeholders* of your system may have special requirements and wishes concerning documentation based upon their specific tasks and experiences.

See Part III, "Appropriateness" on page 159 for further information.

! With the potential exception of *safety critical systems*, completeness is *not* a goal or requirement
● for documentation. In most cases, that would be impossible to achieve and result in overly large or comprehensive documentation.

3.1.2 Exercises

P-question: Your team is constructing and implementing an online eCommerce shop in Java, an object-oriented programming language. A different team will later have the responsibility of maintaining that system, therefore you want to create appropriate architecture documentation. From the list below, which are the *three* most important properties of this architecture documentation in such a case?

Select the *three* most appropriate.

[ ] All classes need to be contained in the documentation.

[x] The documentation must be current and up-to-date.

[x] The documentation should explain the important architecture decisions.

[ ] It contains a complete list of functional requirements.

[ ] It contains a complete list of technical decisions.

[x] It contains the high-priority quality requirements and explains the
     approaches through which these qualities were/are achieved.

3.1.3 References

- [Hargis+2004]: Quality Technical Documentation. A rather long, but highly useful book on technical documentation.

LG 3-2: Describe and communicate software architectures

Describe and communicate software architectures (R1-R3)

Software architects use documentation to support the design, implementation and further development (also called *maintenance* or *evolution*) of systems (R2).

Software architects are able to (R1):

- Document and communicate architectures for corresponding stakeholders, thereby addressing different target groups, e.g. management, development teams, QA, other software architects, and possibly additional stakeholders;
- Consolidate and harmonize the style and content of contributions from different groups of authors;
- Develop and implement measures to support the convergence of written and verbal communication, and balance one against the other appropriately.

Software architects know (R1):

- The benefits of template-based documentation;
- That various properties of documentation depend on specific properties of the system, its requirements, risks, development process, organization or other factors.

For example, software architects can adjust the following documentation characteristics according to the situation (R3):

- The amount and level of detail of documentation needed;
- The documentation format;
- The accessibility of the documentation;
- Formality of documentation (e.g. diagrams compliant to a metamodel or simple drawings);
- Formal reviews and sign-off processes for documentation.

3.2.1 Explanation

The value of architecture documentation

Having the source code of a medium to large system is not enough to understand its structure and concepts. Therefore, some documentation is needed in the long run to facilitate or enable future changes.

Some examples of aspects that are not contained or not well-covered in source code are:

- Overall *structure*: It's difficult or impossible to convey large-scale structure within source code;
- *Architecture decisions:* This could include choices of technologies, structures, patterns, conventions and implementation style;
- *Reasons* for architectural decisions: Why did the team implement this element in the way it did? Why didn't the team choose another solution?

- Technology *choices*: Examples include frameworks or libraries - a subset of architectural decisions;
- *Cross-cutting* concepts: These are used or applied at various locations in source code or configuration.

Stakeholder-specific documentation

Different stakeholders or target groups can have different documentation requirements.

Software architects need to take these into account and help to create documentation that fulfills the needs of these stakeholders, concerning:
- Format (wiki, single document, multiple documents);
- Style (text, diagram or a mixture);
- Structure (based upon generic template, specific structure);
- Notation (e.g. UML);
- Depth;
- Representation (paper or online).

Benefits of templates for architecture documentation

A template for documentation provides a fixed *structure*. Specific documents derived from the template therefore have a uniform structure.

Using such a template for documentation (e.g. [arc42] for software architecture or Volere[28]) provides the following advantages:
- *Understandability* is improved, at least for people aware of the structure. The structure of arc42, for example, is highly optimized for *readability*.
- People new to a system are taken from a bird's eye perspective and fundamental requirements to detailed technical decisions in tiny steps.
- *Retrievability* that enables somebody who knows the overall structure to easily find the desired information.
- It is feasible to *re-use* appropriate parts of the documentation in other systems.
- *Lower effort to maintain* documentation meaning that somebody who is aware of the template structure will easily find the appropriate location to insert or maintain a specific piece of information that needs to be documented.

Documentation depends on many factors

Documentation is a great example of *appropriateness*. See Part III, "Appropriateness" on page 161.

Various aspects of documentation depend on the specifics of a system, its requirements, risks, development, organization and other factors.

These aspects include at least the following:

- Whether written or verbal communication should be prioritized;
- The amount of documentation needed at a particular stage of development;
- Formats and accessibility of documentation;
- Formality of documentation (e.g. diagrams compliant to a metamodel or simple drawings);
- Formal reviews and sign-offs for documentation.

The value of discussing and talking

It's generally regarded as good practice to discuss certain architecture decisions between several of the involved stakeholders and/or within the development team. The involvement of several people avoids bias or operational blindness and usually leads to better decisions in terms of content. The downside of such discussions is that their results are volatile and may be forgotten if they are not made or kept persistently.

Therefore it is necessary to document certain information about the system and its architecture. You need to keep some information about the system in writing and/or drawing. Such *documentation* can be provided on paper, online, or on digital or analog media.

! Software architecture documentation complements *talking* about, or *discussing* software architectures.

When to talk, when to write?

The level of documentation required depend greatly on the system and its organizational context.

Therefore we cannot give general advice, only some heuristics:

- In highly Agile and Lean development of systems with low to moderate criticality (e.g. no human lives are endangered), written documentation might be sparse.
- Volatile teams require more documentation, stable teams can cope with rudimentary documentation.
- In case of safety-critical systems, please comply with the appropriate standards. Documentation and formal reviews are highly important.

3.2.2 Exercises

K-question: Three architects and seventeen developers are working on the documentation of the software architecture for a large system.

Which methods are appropriate in order to achieve a consistent and adequate documentation, and which are not?

Appropriate	Not appropriate	
[x]	[ ]	Templates are used for the documentation.
[ ]	[x]	The chief architect creates the whole documentation.
[x]	[ ]	Certain parts of the documentation are automatically extracted or generated from the source code.
[ ]	[x]	The complete documentation is generated from the source code.

K-question: Which of the following statements are good reasons for maintaining (adequate) architecture documentation and which are not good reasons?

Good reason	Not good reason	
[x]	[ ]	To enable onboarding of new developers.
[x]	[ ]	To conform to legal constraints or requirements.
[x]	[ ]	To support the work of distributed teams.
[x]	[ ]	To assist in future enhancements of the system.

K-question: You can communicate aspects of your software architecture in writing and/or verbally. How are these variants related to each other? Decide for each of the following statements whether it is true or false.

true	false	
[x]	[ ]	Oral communication should complement written documentation.
[ ]	[x]	Written documentation should always precede verbal communication.
[ ]	[x]	Architects should decide on a variant (written or verbal) and then strictly follow this path during development.

3.2.3 References

- [arc42] is an open source, pragmatic and easy-to-use template for software architecture documentation.

LG 3-3: Models and notations to describe software architecture

> **Explain and apply notations/models to describe software architecture (R2-R3)**
>
> Software architects know at least the following UML diagrams to describe architectural views:
> - Class, package, component (all R2) and composite-structure diagrams (R3);
> - Deployment diagrams (R2);
> - Sequence and activity diagrams (R2);
> - State machine diagrams (R3).
>
> Software architects know alternative notations to UML diagrams, for example: (R3)
> - ArchiMate[29]
> - For runtime views, for example flow charts, numbered lists or business-process-modeling-notation (BPMN).

3.3.1 Explanation

UML, the *Universal Modeling Language*, provides a standardized and (very) rich collection of diagram types, plus an extensive metamodel. In simple, terms a metamodel is a *model of a model*. The UML metamodel describes what is allowed in UML models. You can use the metamodel to decide if a specific diagram complies with the UML standard or not.

> ❗ It is not required to know details of the UML metamodel. However, you should have a general idea of several UML diagram types, mentioned below!

Static UML diagrams

Class-, package- and component-diagrams plus composite-structure-diagrams can be used to describe the static structure of a system.

They show white box views, and contain building blocks (static elements of the architecture) plus their dependencies:
- Static elements usually represent any kind of text, source code or configuration, sometimes also non-textual information like diagrams.
- Examples of such static elements are components, classes, functions, modules, packages, services, controllers, configuration-files, stylesheets, markup-files, database-definitions, business-rules or similar.
- A static diagram details the *structure* of a larger element. Every diagram therefore is a white box representation of a higher-level black box.
- A diagram contains *black boxes* (usually drawn as some kind of rectangles) plus their *dependencies* (usually drawn as lines or arrows).
- Depending on the diagram type, these elements (rectangles and lines) have different semantics.

---

29 https://www.opengroup.org/archimate-forum/archimate-overview

In general, the use of UML diagrams is *not* limited to object-oriented programming or -development. UML diagrams can be used to depict the structure and the behavior of arbitrary systems!

Class-, package- and component diagrams

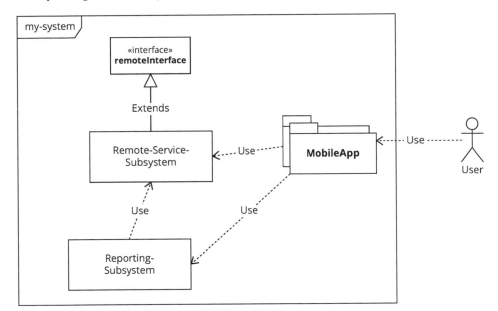

Figure 3.1 Class diagram example

Class diagrams usually contain class symbols.

They can be used to denote classes from object-oriented programming, like in C#, C++ or Java. In principle, you could use class symbols to represent arbitrary architectural elements that are not even related to objects or classes at all.

In our personal opinion you should not use class symbols outside of object-oriented languages in order to avoid any confusion. In case you want to represent some low-level construct (like a C function, configuration file, data-definition or similar), we suggest the use of either package or component symbols instead, with appropriate annotations. See below for details.

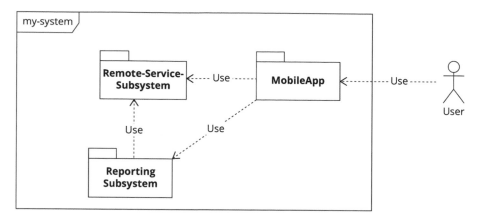

Figure 3.2 Package diagram example

Packages are *bundles* of related elements.

They contain *things* that belong together for certain criteria, but those criteria themselves do not appear in the diagram. The architects or development teams are responsible for defining these criteria.

Be aware that some programming languages, like Java or C#, contain package constructs on a language level. In systems built in these languages you should avoid using the package notation for different things.

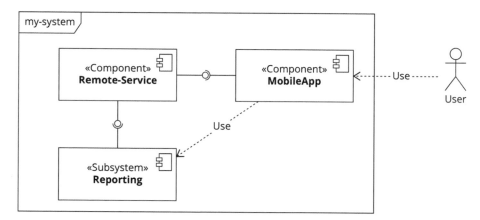

Figure 3.3 Component diagram example

Components can serve multiple purposes in UML diagrams. They can either represent a group or collection of elements, or something atomic. Components can have an explicitly defined interface to one more other component(s).

From our personal experience, components are the most versatile and useful UML constructs for static diagrams, as you can flexibly scale their level of detail. If you need a precise interface, you can enhance the appropriate component by interface- or port constructs. Components can have runtime instances, so you can re-use these components in your deployment diagrams.

! In UML you can use either class, package or component symbols to represent static elements
● (building blocks) of an architecture. You can mix these symbols (*classifiers* in UML terminology)
in diagrams.

To summarize, the following UML symbols can be used to model and depict static elements of your
architecture, see Figure 3.4.

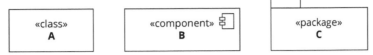

Figure 3.4 UML symbols for static architecture elements

Composite structure diagrams

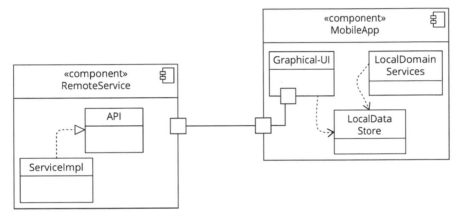

Figure 3.5 Composite structure diagram example

Composite structure diagrams show the internal structure of multiple classes and the interactions
between them. You can graphically represent an internal structure and show associations both
between and within elements. A composite structure diagram is similar to a class diagram, but it can
show individual parts instead of whole classes.

Composite structure diagrams mix black box and white box abstraction of architectural elements.

Dynamic UML diagrams

Dynamic diagrams show behavior at *runtime*. These kinds of diagrams can refer to the system as a
whole, to single or multiple of its elements.

They show (for example):

* Sequences or steps of activities or processes the system performs - either internally or in collaboration with external entities.
* States the system or certain parts of it can reach during execution, or as a reaction to certain events.

Sequence diagrams

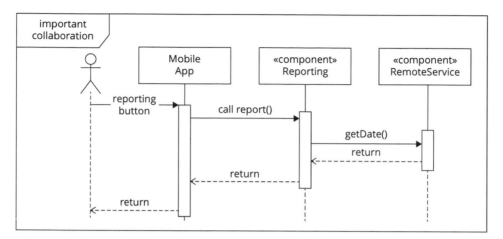

Figure 3.6 Sequence diagram example

Sequence diagrams show how operations are carried out. They contain the interaction between architectural elements or objects in the context of a specific collaboration scenario. Sequence diagrams show the order of the interaction visually by using the vertical x-axis of the diagram to represent time. The boxes in the top represent architectural elements (objects, components). Arrows with solid lines represent method or function calls, or invocations. The dashed arrows represent the returns from these invocations or calls.

In the original UML specification, sequence diagrams depict the collaboration of object-instances, instances of classes within an object-oriented system. In our opinion they can be used to show the collaboration of arbitrary elements of the architecture: building blocks, components, modules, packages, functions or objects.

Activity diagrams

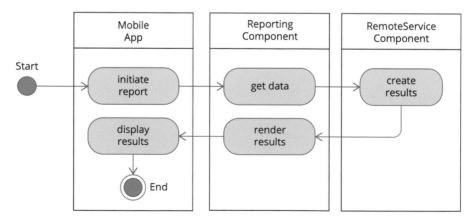

Figure 3.7 Activity diagram example with swim lanes

Activity diagrams describe dynamic aspects of the system, without referring to specific architectural elements. An activity diagram is essentially an advanced version of the simple flow charts.

You can, though, enhance activity diagrams by so called *swim lanes*: they can be used to associate activities with specific elements of the architecture, like components, packages or classes. In our example, the swim lanes represent the MobileApp, the Reporting- and the Remote-Service components.

State machine diagrams

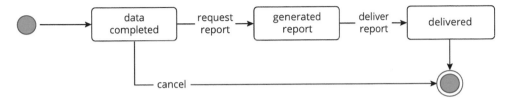

Figure 3.8 State machine diagram example

State machine diagrams (or state diagrams for short) are directed graphs in which rounded rectangular nodes denote *states* and connectors denote *state transitions*.

The initial (first) transition originates from the solid circle and indicates the initial state.

3.3.2 Exercises

K-question: For each of the following statements about static UML diagrams chose if it is true or false.

true	false	
[x]	[ ]	Symbols from UML class- and package diagrams can be used in component diagrams too.
[ ]	[x]	Component diagrams are used to depict the relationship of software to hardware components.
[ ]	[x]	Because of their object-oriented nature, class diagrams are mainly used for runtime models.
[x]	[ ]	Package- and component diagrams should be avoided in software architecture, as they tend to be overly abstract.

P-question: Which four of the following techniques are best suited to illustrate the interaction of architectural elements at runtime?

[x]	Flowcharts.
[ ]	Depiction of screen flows (sequence of user interactions).
[ ]	Linear Venn diagram.
[x]	Sequence diagram.
[x]	Numbered list of sequential steps.

[ ]   Class diagrams.

[x]   Activity diagrams.

[ ]   Tabular description of interfaces.

3.3.3 References

- UML has a very extensive specification (750 pages), not for the fainthearted: https://www.omg.org/spec/UML/2.5.1/PDF
- LG 3-4 explains which diagram type is suited for which particular architectural view.

LG 3-4: Architectural views

Explain and use architectural views (R1)

Software architects are able to use the following architectural views:

- Context view;
- Building block or component view (composition of software building blocks);
- Runtime view (dynamic view, interaction between software building blocks at runtime, state machines);
- Deployment view (hardware and technical infrastructure as well as the mapping of software building blocks onto the infrastructure).

3.4.1 Explanation

As already stated in LG 3-3, knowledge of the UML metamodel is not required for the examination. In particular, the subtle distinction between the numerous types of relationships or associations ("lines and arrows") is not required for the examination.

Context view

For a detailed explanation of the context view, see LG 3-5.

Building block view

Content and motivation

The building block view explains the static decomposition of the system into building blocks (modules, components, subsystems, packages, classes, functions, files ...) and their relationships (interfaces, dependencies, associations, relations. . .). It shows the overall structure of the source code and code-related artifacts, e.g. configuration files, stylesheets or similar things.

This view is usually organized or communicated in a hierarchy of levels, as already described in LG 2-2. The topmost level of the description of your whole IT system (level-0) is documented in the context view which will be described in detail in the next chapter. The first level of internal building blocks (level-1) shows the whole system as a structure of white boxes: the internal subsystems or major parts of the system. Lower levels, if available, drill down into additional details.

Figure 3.9 shows this stepwise refinement from a context view down to a single diagram on level-2.

Please note that on level-2, there could be as many different diagrams as there are building blocks on level-1.

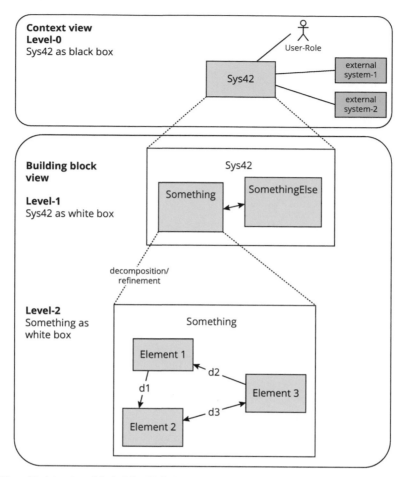

Figure 3.9 Hierarchical structure of the building block view

Form and how-to

As described in LG 3-3, several of the static UML diagram types might be used to depict white box structures: Class, package and component diagrams are well-suited to convey structures.

Diagrams in the building block view show white box structures, an important part of the white box representation of building blocks (see LG 2-2). In addition to the diagram, a white box should contain the *design rationale* and a brief description of the contained → black boxes plus their dependencies. The ideas behind black boxes are treated in LG 2-1.

Runtime view

Content and motivation

The runtime view shows behavior, interactions and runtime dependencies of the building blocks in the form of either generic or concrete scenarios.

It helps you to understand *how* the building blocks of your systems fulfill their respective tasks at runtime, and *how* they communicate and interact with each other at runtime.

Form and how-to

- Enumerated lists;
- Pseudo-code snippets;
- UML sequence diagrams;
- UML activity diagrams with swim lanes indicating the corresponding building blocks;
- UML state transition diagrams;
- UML object diagrams (in our opinion these are not appropriate for real-world scenarios);
- Other dynamic diagrams, like flowcharts.

All runtime diagrams should be amended by textual or tabular descriptions explaining the interactions where necessary.

Example

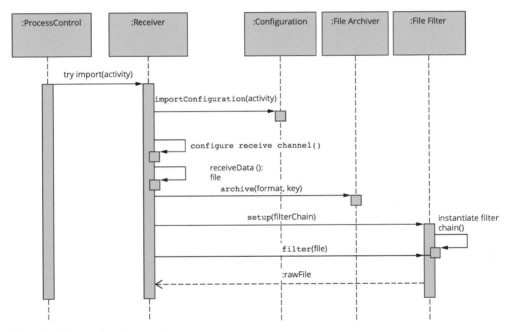

Figure 3.10 Example of runtime scenario

1. tryImport: `ProcessControl` starts the import. The `activity` is a unique ID identifying the mandator, the campaign and the activity.
2. `importConfiguration` gets all required configuration information.
3. `configureReceiveChannel` prepares everything needed to get data from an external source. For example, URL, file names and authentication credentials for an external ftp server need to be configured here.
4. `archive` sends the file to the (configured) archive system, usually an optical write-once non-erasable backup archive.
5. `setup` initializes the required filters, e.g. unzip or decrypt.
6. `filter` executes all the filters.

Steps 5+6 are a dynamically configured pipes-and-filters dataflow subsystem.

Deployment view

Content and motivation

It is important to know the technical infrastructure where your system and its building blocks will be executed. That's especially the case if your software is distributed or deployed on several different machines, application servers or containers. For example, the building block view usually does not tell you whether a component is to be run in the user's browser or on the backend server.

If appropriate, you should explain different environments (like dev, test, production).

Form and how-to

Use UML deployment diagrams with:

- Nodes showing execution environments (hardware, virtualized hardware, processors, application servers or similar environments executing software).
- Edges/channels linking nodes with each other or the environment.
- (Optionally) artifacts, representing your software building blocks in executable form (e.g. compiled and/or packaged).

Deployment diagrams should be amended by a textual or tabular description.

You should explain where your software artifacts are executed. If that information is not contained in the diagrams, you should describe it as text or a table.

Example

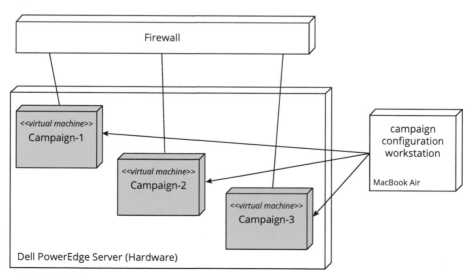

Figure 3.11 MaMa deployment overview

Element	Description
Campaign-i	Virtual machine for one single campaign.

3.4.2 Exercises

K-question: You need to document a large subsystem of your software architecture.

What information should and should not be included in the black box description of this component?

Select the correct choice for each answer option.

shall	shall-not	
[x]	[ ]	Interfaces.
[x]	[ ]	Responsibilities.
[ ]	[x]	Internal structure.
[ ]	[x]	Implementation suggestions.

P-question: Some architecture development methods suggest a *view-based approach*. Which of the following are the *three* most important of such architectural views?

[ ]	Test-driven view.
[x]	Context view.
[x]	Building block/component view.
[ ]	Configuration view.
[x]	Runtime view.
[ ]	Physical database view.

3.4.3 References

- Views have been described in Kruchten's 4+1 model [Kruchten1995]. Kruchten proposes to start with use-case scenarios (the "+1") and use physical (infrastructure), logical, development (building blocks) and process (runtime) view.
- The context view is covered in LG 3-5 in more detail.
- Rozanski and Woods [Rozanski+11] treat architectural viewpoints and perspectives.
- The open source arc42 [arc42] template proposes to use context, building block, runtime and deployment view, and is therefore highly compatible in terminology with iSAQB.

LG 3-5: Context view

Explain and apply context view of systems (R1)

Software architects can:

- Depict the context of systems, e.g. in the form of context diagrams with explanations;
- Represent external interfaces of systems in the context view;
- Differentiate between business and technical context.

3.5.1 Explanation

What is the "context"?

The → context of a system comprises all those parts of the environment that are relevant to the system, including but not limited to its neighbors.

To distinguish between "our system" and "everything else" and describe the relationship between our system and its environment, the context view has to clarify two important aspects:

1. System scope, differentiating between "outside" and "inside" of the system;
2. External interfaces.

> *System scope and context - as the name suggests - delimits your system (i.e. your scope) from all its communication partners (neighboring systems and users, i.e. the context of your system). It thereby specifies the external interfaces.*

Quote from arc42 documentation, https://docs.arc42.org

External interfaces

The interfaces to neighboring systems often belong to the most critical aspects of a system for a number of reasons:

- You (often) have no influence on these external interfaces, their development, evolution or operation. These interfaces might change without your consent, and your system has to deal with such changes.
- Your system's functionality is (often) triggered via external interfaces or via events that originate in the "outside". For example, a user (an external entity from your system's point of view) enters a command in the user interface.
- Negotiating the details of external interfaces (often) takes longer or requires additional stakeholders to participate and agree.
- If end-user functionality requires communication with external systems, their quality properties (like performance, reliability, security) directly influences the qualities of your system. If the external system fails or behaves badly, your system needs to handle such problems.

Business context and technical context

It might be useful to differentiate between business (logical or essential input/output) and technical (channels, technical protocols, hardware) context:

- The *business* context (formerly called *logical* context) shows the external relationships from a business- or non-technical perspective. It abstracts from technical, hardware or implementation details. Input-/output relationships are named by their *business meaning* instead of their technical properties.
- The *technical* context shows technical details, like transmission channel, technical protocol, IP address, bus or similar hardware details. Embedded systems, for example, often care for hardware-related information very early in their development.

Documenting the context view

We propose to use a diagram plus a table to explain the context view:

- Provide a diagram for the overview. Use UML component, package or class diagrams (as described in LG 3-3), or free form diagrams.
- Use a table to explain the elements (especially the external interfaces of the system).

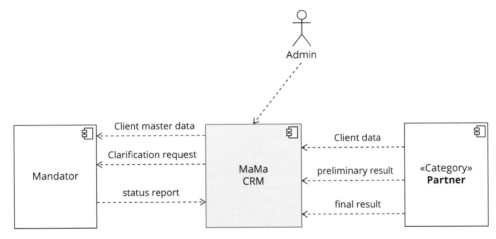

Figure 3.12 Example of a (detailed) business context view

Interface / neighbor system	Exchanged data
Client master data	Mandator transfers client master data to MaMa-CRM, initiating the campaign.

❗ Make sure to include all relevant external systems and the interfaces your system uses or provides in the context view. You can describe the details of these interfaces either here (in the context view), the building block view or even in a cross-cutting concept. However, this is the right place to provide a comprehensive overview.

3.5.2 Exercises

P-question: Pick the *two* most appropriate answers that apply to the technical context.

[x]   The technical context contains the physical channels between your system and its environment.

[ ]   The technical context contains all the infrastructure on which the components of your system are deployed.

[x]   The technical context might contain different elements than the business context.

[ ]   The technical context should include hardware pricing or pricing of cloud services used as infrastructure for your system.

[ ]   The technical context contains information about the chosen programming language used to implement your system.

P-question: Pick the *three* most appropriate answers that apply to the business context.

[x]   The business context contains the business or domain interaction between your system and its neighbors.

[x]   The business context contains the whole system as a black box.

[ ]   The business context shows the internal components of the system as a white box.

[x]   The business context should contain all external interfaces of the system.

[ ]   To facilitate understanding, external neighbor systems can be shown in multiple colors.

3.5.3 References

- The context view is also mentioned in LG 3-4.
- Appropriate UML diagram types are explained in LG 3-3.
- The open source arc42 [arc42] template contains numerous practical tips on how to treat the context view, see https://docs.arc42.org/section-3/.

LG 3-6: Document cross-cutting concepts

Document and communicate cross-cutting concepts (R2)

Software architects are able to adequately document and communicate typical cross-cutting concepts (synonym: *principles, aspects*), e. g., persistence, workflow management, UI, deployment/integration, logging.

3.6.1 Explanation

In LG 2-4 we have already discussed the notion of cross-cutting concerns. This led us to architectural decisions that affect a large number of architectural elements, resulting in the development of cross-cutting concepts. To describe these concepts directly in the involved modules, e.g. in the building block view, would lead to redundant and poorly structured documentation.

Therefore it is advisable to present cross-cutting concepts in a dedicated section of the architecture documentation.

In this way they become a cornerstone of the conceptual integrity of your architecture and ensure that future architectural decisions are made in a consistent manner.

 Since cross-cutting concepts can have a considerable impact on your architectural design, make sure you communicate them adequately to all relevant stakeholders. Especially when they are subject to change.

Most cross-cutting concepts consist of a solution approach in conjunction with specific technology decisions. They often contain technical details, so documenting them in one single central place can contribute to a more compact documentation of the building block view.

Their description should support the implementation by providing explanations and guidelines for the affected building blocks. Give preference to those concepts that are of central significance and document them with diagrams, source code extracts and explanatory texts. Get support from the development team or technology experts as needed, or delegate the task of creating documentation for specific concepts to them.

The level of detail and scope of the documentation may vary. Sometimes a short and concise statement concerning a technology decision is sufficient, e.g. the commitment to a logging or ORM framework. However, more comprehensive descriptions may also be required, e.g. a security concept with typical threat scenarios and suitable solutions. Using a template that can be customized to your needs might prove to be useful. It can or should contain the following sections:

- **Purpose**: Problem to be solved by the cross-cutting concept and particular requirements.
- **Constraints**: Which constraints and restrictions have to be considered?
- **Solution strategy**: Provide examples of the solution, preferably with source code ("reference implementation"). If necessary, explain related structures and processes.

- **References and additional resources**: Many standard solutions with ample documentation exist and it is more efficient to refer to them than to document them yourself.
- **Risks**: Point out possible risks, trade-offs or side-effects.
- **Rejected alternatives**: If potential alternative solutions have been rejected, you should mention them and explain your decision.

Examples of cross-cutting concepts

Some examples will help to clarify what could be covered in such concepts:

- If several of your building blocks (another term for components or modules) need to be structured in a similar way, you could specify or prescribe an appropriate architecture - or design pattern - for these elements.
- If your system contains several different *forms* within a graphical user interface, you could specify or prescribe the way in which such forms are designed (from a layout perspective), structured and implemented (from a code perspective) and tested by providing a cross-cutting concept.
- If a system needs to implement several *reports* on existing data, you could standardize the way such reports are generated by prescribing a uniform approach to data collection, calculation, and the layout/rendering of results, etc.
- You may provide a crosscutting-concept on how data privacy or similar IT-security concerns/ aspects are handled within the system and related processes.

The open source arc42 template contains around 30 typical candidates for cross-cutting concepts: https://docs.arc42.org/section-8/

3.6.2 Exercises

P-question: Which *four* of the following statements about (cross-cutting) concepts are most appropriate?

[x]	Such concepts are a means to increase consistency.
[ ]	Uniform usage of concepts reduces coupling between building blocks.
[x]	Uniform exception handling is most easily achieved when architects agree with developers upon a suitable concept prior to implementation.
[x]	A concept might be implemented by a single building block.
[ ]	The definition of cross-cutting concepts ensures the ISO-25010 compliance of the architecture.
[x]	A concept can define constraints for the implementation of many building blocks.
[ ]	For each quality goal there should be an explicitly documented concept.

P-question: Software architecture documentation could contain descriptions of cross-cutting concepts. Pick the TWO best reasons why documentation of cross-cutting concepts is useful.

[ ]   Cross-cutting concepts should focus on the domain and be free of technical information.

[x]   Aspects or concepts that are used in multiple parts of your software architecture should be described in a non-redundant way.

[x]   Cross-cutting concepts can be reused in more products within the same organization.

[ ]   Cross-cutting concepts should be implemented by specialists. Therefore, separate documentation is useful.

3.6.3 References

LG 2-4 also deals with cross-cutting concepts.

LG 3-7: Describe interfaces

Describe interfaces (R1)
Software architects are able to describe and specify both internal and external interfaces.

3.7.1 Explanation

In this context, the term → interface refers to the shared boundary between two or more components across which they interact.

In LG 2-9 we have already covered the design and definition of interfaces. More often than not, well designed and documented internal and external interfaces can form the backbone of a maintainable architecture. However, specifying and documenting interfaces can be a daunting task that can require a great deal of effort. The necessary level of detail and extent of the documentation to be provided will depend on the specific context in each individual case. For interfaces that are accessed by a large number of (external) users or that have to be coordinated with a "difficult" external contractor, then more concise and detailed documentation is advisable. Some stakeholders may even require stand-alone interface documentation.

Accordingly, it is best to pay sufficient attention to the documentation of interfaces in early stages of a project, as long as things can still be changed and adapted with little effort. If necessary, plan ahead for API evolution and interface versioning.

A lightweight but highly efficient resource for documentation are test cases and sample code. Appropriate tool support (e.g. Swagger[30]) or the use of interface description languages (IDLs) can also be beneficial. You might even want to design interfaces that they are self-describing in the way HATEOAS[31] (Hypermedia as the Engine of Application State) works. As always, "it Depends". Even if this is no substitute for documentation, it improves the learnability and comprehensibility of interfaces considerably.

In any case, you should consider providing a template for the documentation of interfaces that addresses the following points:
- **Identification**: Name and version of the interface.
- **Provided resources**: Syntax and semantics of the provided resources.
- **Impact and side effects**: Which impact does a call of a resource have? What data is changed? Does the state change or are events triggered? Are there any other side effects?
- **Errors**: What error conditions can occur? How are errors communicated and handled? What types of errors exist? What consequences does the occurrence of errors have on the affected component? How should a client react to an error condition?

---

30 https://swagger.io/
31 https://en.wikipedia.org/wiki/HATEOAS

- **Constraints:** Which restrictions or constraints exist on the use of a resource? Are there any pre- or post-conditions?
- **Quality attributes:** Which (non-trivial) quality attributes or requirements are tied to the use of resources? (e.g. performance, response time, load, memory usage, …).
- **Design decisions:** Important design decisions and possibly rejected alternatives.
- **Stability/evolution:** How stable is this interface? Is there a roadmap for future changes? Which functions are deprecated? What were breaking changes from the previous version of this interface?
- **Additional information:** Notes, "should knows" and usage examples.

3.7.2 Exercises

K-question: What are guidelines for good interface design? Check which of the following statements are true and which are false.

true	false	
[x]	[ ]	Use of interfaces should be easy to learn from a consumer/client perspective.
[ ]	[x]	An interface should always be defined by the provider of the appropriate service.
[x]	[ ]	Interface specifications should contain functional and non-functional aspects.
[x]	[ ]	The client code should be easy to understand.

3.7.3 References

- LG 2-9 covers designing and defining interfaces.

In our opinion, the topic of "methodical interface design" belongs to the *open issues* in software engineering.

One brief summary of good practices is:

- Bloch, Joshua: How to Design a Good API and Why it Matters. TechTalk at Google, available online at: https://fwdinnovations.net/whitepaper/APIDesign.pdf.
  Josh Bloch is the designer of the well-known Java Collection framework.

Several recent books cover the specific topic of web-API design:

- Kirsten Hunter's "Irresistible APIs" [Hunter2016];
- API Design Patterns from J. J. Geewax [Geewax2020].

LG 3-8: Document architectural decisions

Explain and document architectural decisions (R1-R2)

Software architects are able to:

- Systematically take, justify, communicate, and document architectural decisions;
- Identify, communicate, and document the interdependencies between design decisions.

Software architects know about Architecture Decision Records (ADR, see [Nygard2011]) and can apply these to document decisions (R2).

3.8.1 Explanation

Architectural decisions are any decisions within the software/system architecture that concern architecturally significant requirements. Often such decisions are perceived as hard to take and/or hard to change (see [Fowler2003]). Architectural decisions often affect the fundamental structure, quality characteristics, external interfaces or fundamental construction techniques, principles, and concepts (as defined by Michael Nygard [Nygard2011]).

How to take architectural decisions

There is no systematic answer on taking decisions. You need architectural knowledge and should consider at least the following aspects:

- Explicitly state *what* you want or need to decide - maybe even *why* it must be decided.
- Explicitly formulate the appropriate quality requirements that are related to the decision.
- Be especially aware of safety requirements.
- What functional requirements are involved?
- What solution approaches are already known or implemented?
- Consider the technical constraints, what technologies are available or feasible?
- Take the current organizational constraints into account, including the team, the budget and the available timeframe.
- Who is affected by this decision?

With these (and maybe more) prerequisites covered, you should come up with at least two different alternatives.

For each alternative try to formulate:

- What assumptions have you made?
- What are the specific advantages?
- What are the specific disadvantages?
- What compromises or consequences arise from each alternative?
- What are the known or estimated costs of each alternative?

Architecture decision records

An Architecture Decision Record (ADR) is a *template* to document an architectural decision.

According to Michael Nygard [Nygard2011] it should consist of the following parts:
- **Title**: Preferably containing a unique ADR identifier.
- **Status**: What is the status, e.g. proposed, accepted, rejected, deprecated, superseded, etc.?
- **Context**: What is the issue that we're seeing that is motivating this decision or change?
- **Decision**: What is the change that we're proposing and/or doing?
- **Consequences**: What becomes easier or more difficult to do because of this change?

This information should be kept together, either in a distinct text file, or at a specific location within your architecture documentation.

3.8.2 Exercises

Reflect on the relationships and potential dependencies of different architectural decisions.

How can architectural decisions influence each other? Can you name examples where:
- One decision lays the foundations for the next?
- One decision makes the next difficult or impossible?

How could the relationships between decisions be documented? How could ADRs be used for such inter-decision relationships?

K-question: One definition says: "Software architecture is the sum of all the decisions you have taken during development." Check which of the following statements about architectural/design decisions are true and which are false.

true	false	
[x]	[ ]	Architectural decisions can be implicitly contained in the structure of the building block/ component view.
[ ]	[x]	Software architects should justify all design decisions in writing.
[x]	[ ]	Architectural decisions can have interdependencies between each other.
[x]	[ ]	Tradeoffs between conflicting quality requirements should be explicit decisions.

3.8.3 References

- See https://en.wikipedia.org/wiki/Architectural_decision on architectural decisions.
- Architecture Decision Records (ADR) see [Nygard2011].
- See the curated list of references concerning ADR on https://adr.github.io/
- Joel Parker Henderson provides information on ADRs and templates on https://github.com/joelparkerhenderson/architecture_decision_record.
- [Zimmermann+2015] have created an (academic) overview of architectural decision guidance.

LG 3-9: Resources and tools for documentation

Know additional resources and tools for documentation (R3)

Software architects know:

- Basics of several published frameworks for the description of software architectures, for example ISO/IEEE-42010 (formerly 1471) [ISO-42010], arc42 [arc42], C4 [Brown-C4], or FMC [Wendt-FMC];
- Ideas and examples of checklists for the creation, documentation and testing of software architectures;
- Possible tools for creating and maintaining architectural documentation.

3.9.1 Explanation

❗ This learning goal is not relevant for the examination.

In practice you need tools to create and maintain documentation both efficiently and effectively. Your concrete set of tools strongly depends on organizational and technical constraints (like company-wide standards you have to comply with), the kind and size of your system, your development team(s), other involved stakeholders and so forth.

Methodical tools for documentation

Our pragmatic approach to software architecture documentation is based on arc42 [arc42], a flexible and well-established open source documentation template.

Technical tools for documentation

You have a number of options that can be used to document your software architectures:

Examples:

- Modelling tools, e.g. UML modelling. Such tools rely on the established UML modelling notation, resulting in a defined model and diagram syntax. Tools tend to be powerful yet quite complicated or difficult to use.
- Wiki systems focus on collaboration. Multiple users can share documentation and collaborate easily on their creation and management. Wikis are usually restricted to textual or tabular documentations, diagrams are added by plugins.
- Office tools are widely available, allowing for combinations of text, tables and diagrams. Collaboration between several users might be quite limited.
- Plain-text documentation (like Markdown, AsciiDoc or Textile) regard documentation as just another artifact on a par with source code. Documentation is usually versioned within the source repository (e.g. Git, subversion or similar version control systems).

Tools for testing software architectures

Again, various categories of tools can help you test and verify several aspects of your architecture:

- Static analysis tools can determine metrics like code complexity, analyze dependencies and coupling, and ensure adherence to coding rules and standards. Some of these tools are open source, like SonarQube (see below), with commercial support.
- Some architectural properties (like dependencies, naming of components, applied stereotypes, compliance to a layer structure etc.) can be automatically *tested* together with other unit tests. An example of such a tool is ArchUnit.
- Dedicated architecture analysis tools, e.g. Structure101, SonarGraph, Sotograph and others, can help in a what-if kind of analysis. Many of them can visualize dependencies, in order to obtain an overview.
- Some programming languages provide *linters* (static code analysis tools used to detect programming errors, bugs, stylistic errors and suspicious constructs). Linters are common for Unix programming, JavaScript, the Go programming language and others.

Disclaimer: The authors are not affiliated with any of the tools mentioned here.

The list given is by no means complete.

3.9.2 References

- Cyrille Martraire: Living Documentation [Martraire2019].
- Docs-as-Code, an approach to include architecture documentation close to the source code. https://docs-as-co.de/
- SonarQube, https://www.sonarsource.com/products/sonarqube/, an open source analysis tool with plugins for many programming languages.
- ArchUnit, https://archunit.org, an open source library for testing architectural constraints. Available for the Java platform and C#.

CPSA-F Chapter 4: Software architecture and quality

LG 4-1: Quality models and quality characteristics

Discuss quality models and quality characteristics (R1)

Software architects can explain:
- The concept of quality and quality characteristics (based on e.g. ISO 25010 or [Bass+2021]);
- Generic quality models (such as ISO 25010, [Bass+2021], or [Q42];
- Correlations and trade-offs of quality characteristics, for example:
  - configurability versus reliability;
  - memory requirements versus performance efficiency;
  - security versus usability;
  - runtime flexibility versus maintainability.

4.1.1 Explanation

Quality

The term "quality" is used in everyday life in a very imprecise and subjective manner. It denotes something "good", usually without any additional specification. Transferring this term to software development carries several risks or problems:
- Quality can have different meanings for different people. One person aims mainly for performance, whereas another considers security or portability to be more important.
- Different stakeholders might have different needs or opinions concerning specific quality attributes. The performance required by one person may not be good enough for another.
- People often have *implicit* assumptions about their quality requirements, which makes it difficult for development teams to achieve the desired properties.
- As the term "quality" is often used without further specification in real-life, it is often (wrongly!) assumed, that everybody has the same interpretation of "high quality".

Quality is more than a single property or attribute of any given system. Rather, quality is a generic term and needs to be specified or described by using more detailed or precise terms.

Quality should be understood as a set of desired, required or given properties of a system. Examples are *runtime performance*, *robustness* and *portability*.

Quality attribute(s)

The various "properties" or aspects of quality are either called

- quality *attributes*;
- quality *properties*; or
- quality *characteristics*.

These terms might be used interchangeably.

Quality model

To enable a more structured and uniform view on "software quality", researchers came up with (pragmatic) "quality models":

A software quality model is a collection of attributes (properties, characteristics) that software systems might have or need to have. There has been extensive discussion in academia on such models in the 1980's (so don't bother!), that finally ended up in an ISO standard (ISO/OSI 9126) - which described a hierarchical, generic quality model. ISO-9126 has been superseded by the ISO-25010 family of standards describing software quality.

Such quality models collect and structure a number of typical properties or attributes of software systems. The diagram in Figure 4.1 contains the top-level quality attributes or quality characteristics from ISO-25010:

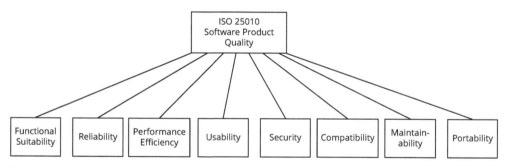

Figure 4.1 ISO 25010 top level quality attributes

Hierarchical quality models break down their top-level properties into finer grained properties - sometimes called sub-attributes, sub-properties, or in case of ISO-25010 quality sub-characteristics.

Figure 4.2 shows the full ISO 25010 tree of software product quality attributes.

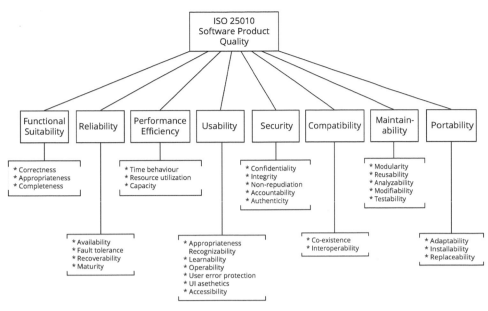

Figure 4.2 ISO 25010

❗ It is not required to memorize the content or definition of this ISO standard! You should understand the hierarchical structure of these models: Top-level properties are broken down into
sub-properties.

Typical conflicts between quality requirements

It might seem obvious, but in most cases you cannot achieve every desired quality attribute, as some
properties inherently conflict with others.

Let's consider some examples:

- Robustness ("stability") versus runtime flexibility (i.e. configurability): Runtime configuration
  makes testing much more difficult, if not impossible. Potentially dangerous configuration options
  might lead to runtime problems. In theory, you could eliminate such problems by sophisticated
  runtime checking of that configuration, but this would definitely increase the complexity of your
  system.
- Memory requirements versus performance efficiency: In a case where a system is highly restricted
  in memory (e.g. an embedded system with only 512kbyte of memory), then it is likely to work
  slower (e.g. it cannot cache many results and needs to garbage-collect or free-up its memory more
  often).
- IT-security versus usability: Security is often achieved by user-specific logins, access restrictions and limiting functionality for non-authenticated users. These security measures inherently
  require the user to carry out certain activities, like login and authentication, which definitely don't
  contribute to ease-of-use or a pleasing user experience. Therefore it's widely accepted that security
  conflicts to some extent with usability or user-experience.
- Sometimes runtime performance conflicts with understandability or simplicity: Imagine your
  system needs to access a database. To optimize read performance, you implement preloading and

caching, so users get some results a lot quicker. The downside of this kind of performance optimization is increased complexity, as caching, cache-invalidation, caching-strategies and cache-synchronization are algorithmically difficult problems and will surely increase the complexity of your source code - making it less understandable.

Trade-offs or compromises between quality attributes

As described in the preceding section, several quality attributes influence each other. Nearly every quality property requires more time and/or money to implement. In reality, architects and development teams have to find proper trade-offs between the different quality requirements.

! A trade-off balances several desirable but incompatible features. Another term for trade-off is "compromise". For example, "a trade-off between performance and time-to-market".

4.1.2 Exercises

K-question: Which of the following pairs of quality attributes are often in conflict with each other, and which are not?

conflicting	not conflicting	
[x]	[ ]	Runtime configurability and robustness.
[ ]	[x]	Understandability and readability.
[ ]	[x]	Security and legal compliance.
[x]	[ ]	Usability and security.

4.1.3 References

- LG 4-2 shows how to clarify generic quality requirements, how to specify the generic terms for concrete systems.
- LG 4-3 explains methods to analyze or evaluate the quality properties of systems.
- The Software Engineering Institute (SEI) has written extensively on software quality, see https://resources.sei.cmu.edu/library/asset-view.cfm?assetid=513803

LG 4-2: Clarify quality requirements

Clarify quality requirements for software architectures (R1)

Software architects can:

- Clarify and formulate specific quality requirements for the software to be developed and its architectures, for example in the form of scenarios and quality trees;
- Explain and apply scenarios and quality trees.

4.2.1 Explanation

Prior to reading this explanation, you need to understand the following terms, all of which are covered in LG-4-1:

- quality;
- quality attribute;
- quality model.

Quality scenarios

Quality scenarios document and clarify the required quality attributes. They help to describe required or desired *qualities* of a system in a pragmatic and informal manner, making the abstract term "quality" more concrete, specific and tangible.

Consider the following examples of quality scenarios:

- An authenticated user requests generation of the daily sales report in PDF format via the graphical user interface. The system generates this report in less than 10 seconds.
- When a user configures a health insurance contract, the system calculates a price estimate based on the currently available information. This estimate must be within a ±15% margin relative to the final price.
- The user registration service must be available 7x24h 99%.
- A new insurance tariff can be implemented in the system in less than 10 days.
- A service crashed at runtime. It can be restarted to fully operational state in less than 30 seconds.

See the diagram below for a schematic overview on the structure and contents of a quality scenario:

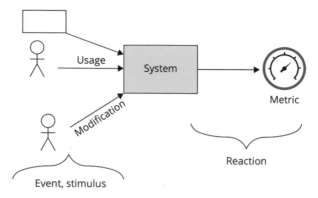

Figure 4.3 Schematic quality scenario

- **Event/stimulus:** Any condition or event arriving at the system.
- **Response:** The activity undertaken after the arrival of the stimulus.
- **System (or part of the system):** Some artifact is stimulated, which may be the whole system or some distinct pieces (artifacts) of it.
- **Metric (response measure):** The response should be measurable in some fashion, so that this scenario (quality requirement) can be objectively assessed or *tested*.

The use of quality scenarios as a means to document and specify quality requirements has been proposed by the Software Engineering Institute (SEI), see Appendix C References.

There are different types of scenarios:
1. **Usage scenarios:** The system is used (any use case or system function is executed). Such scenarios describe how the system *behaves* in these cases, e.g. in terms of runtime performance, memory consumption, throughput or similar. They are also known as application scenarios.
2. **Change scenarios:** Any component within the system, its environment or its operational infrastructure changes or is being changed. They are also called modification or growth scenarios.
3. **Failure scenarios:** Some part of the system, its infrastructure or neighbors fail. Other terms for these types of scenario are boundary, stress, or exploratory scenarios.

Quality tree

The official term of the SEI is *quality attribute utility tree*, but we abbreviate that to *quality tree* for the sake of simplicity. On the root of this tree you usually keep the term *quality*. In the top branches, you break quality down into several quality attributes, the attributes into sub-attributes. At the leaves of the tree, you find scenarios.

The easiest way to understand such a tree is a short example, as in Figure 4.4. Please note: This resembles the tree structure of the ISO 25010 [ISO-25010], which is explained in LG-4-1, but the ISO norm does not contain detailed quality scenarios and it is not specific to your system. Hence the use of the term "specific quality tree" for this means of describing required or already established qualities of your IT system.

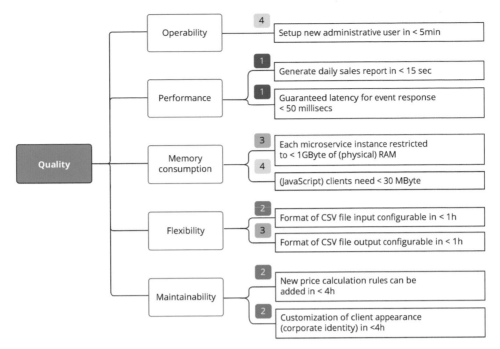

Figure 4.4 Example of a quality tree

4.2.2 Exercises

Try to find concrete or specific expressions for some quality requirements of a system you know about.

Formulate a scenario for the following quality attributes:

- Time to market (the time needed from initial specification of a requirement until the system is productive);
- Runtime performance;
- Robustness and availability;
- Ease-of-use (hint: imagine a graphical user interface and a person trying to achieve a specific result with the system).

P-question: ISO 25010 provides generic quality characteristics for software systems. How can quality requirements concerning these characteristics be made more concrete? Pick the *two* best alternatives.

[ ]   By defining explicit interfaces.

[x]   By creating a specific quality tree.

[ ]   By developing UI prototypes.

[ ]   By creating automatic tests.

[x]   By discussing or writing scenarios.

4.2.3 References

- Quality scenarios have been invented by authors from the Software Engineering Institute (SEI), see for example [Bass+2021] or online
  https://resources.sei.cmu.edu/library/asset-view.cfm?assetid=513803
- LG 4-1 introduces the term "quality" plus several other related terms.
- LG 4-3 explains methods to analyze or evaluate the quality properties of systems.

LG 4-3: Qualitative analysis

Qualitative analysis of software architectures (R2-R3)

Software architects:

- Know methodical approaches for the qualitative analysis of software architectures (R2), for example, as specified by ATAM (R3);
- Can qualitatively analyze smaller systems (R2);
- Know that the following sources of information can help in the qualitative analysis of architectures (R2):
  - quality requirements, e.g. in the form of quality trees and scenarios;
  - architecture documentation;
  - architecture and design models;
  - source code;
  - metrics;
  - other documentation of the system, such as requirements, operational or test documentation.

4.3.1 Explanation

A well-known and respected approach for the qualitative evaluation of software architecture is ATAM, the *Architecture Tradeoff Analysis Method*, invented and published by the Software Engineering Institute, see also [Kazman+2000].

> **!** For the examination, only general knowledge of qualitative analysis methods is required. Details of the ATAM method are *not relevant* for the examination.

We introduce a simplified (and rather pragmatic) version of ATAM, which concentrates on the core steps. The original ATAM consists of a nine step process that is described in detail by the SEI in their documentation. You'll need that extensive version if you apply ATAM to very large systems or in safety-critical situations.

Qualitative analysis and evaluation

 A brief analysis, as described below, might not be sufficient in critical situations, especially where safety-critical systems are concerned!

1. Create clear and tangible *quality requirements* that can be operationalized. Quality scenarios (see the corresponding section in LG 4-2) are a great way of doing this. This step requires the cooperation of stakeholders.
2. Find out what architectural approaches have been decided or implemented to support these quality requirements. This step requires deep architectural understanding of the system to be evaluated.
3. Compare the architectural approaches to the quality requirements in order to analyze if the approaches can possibly work, or might fail. Identify risks or problems in the architecture or its implementation with respect to the specific quality requirements described in step 1.

To understand qualitative analysis, you need to grasp some fundamental terms, namely quality, quality model, quality scenario and quality tree, covered in sections LG-4-1 and LG-4-2.

What does a qualitative analysis deliver?

Any qualitative analysis or evaluation will deliver the following results:

- Quality requirements in terms of a **quality tree** (with scenarios). In most cases, these scenarios will be prioritized.
- **Risks** with respect to the scenarios. Risky scenarios are not adequately addressed by the architecture. There is a danger that this scenario will not be satisfied by the system.
- **Non-risks:** What quality scenarios have been adequately addressed by the architecture or the implementation. These scenarios will most certainly be satisfied by the system.
- **Trade-offs** (also known as *compromises*) between conflicting goals, e.g. what trade-off or compromise has been made between security and usability.
- **Sensitivity points** (optional): Which scenarios are only just met or may no longer be safely achieved when changes are made to the IT system.

 For practical software architecture work we strongly suggest the development of *quality scenarios* as early as possible. A good starting point are requirements clarification activities.

Which artifacts can be useful in qualitative analysis?

! The following artifacts or activities might be useful when you conduct a qualitative analysis:

- **Quality requirements** which form the basis for the analysis because they represent the standard or benchmark against which we can evaluate. The well-known ATAM method proposes that you should develop these requirements as first step in the analysis as a (prioritized) quality tree with scenarios. See LG-4-2 for details.
- **Architecture documentation** provides an overview of the solution approach. You might use this documentation to verify if certain quality requirements will likely fail (*risks*) or can easily be met (*non-risks*).
- **Architecture and design models:** same as architecture documentation.
- **Source code** provides the utmost level of detail. Code should be consulted when no documentation is available or when documentation is outdated.
- **Metrics**, e.g. static or dynamic metrics, can provide indicators concerning numerous quality characteristics, like flexibility, maintainability, understandability, complexity or performance.
- **Other documentation**, such as requirements, operational or test documentation and test results.
- **Stakeholder interviews** help to locate known issues or problems with the system.

Who can or should participate in qualitative analysis?

Representatives of the following groups should, if possible, be involved when performing qualitative analysis:

- Evaluator(s): One or several people knowledgeable in software architecture who will independently analyze the architecture. Having people from outside the development team perform the analysis helps to get unbiased results.
- Business or product owners: People who know the requirements of the systems are needed to derive and prioritize the current quality requirements.
- Software architect(s): People who know about the architecture and design decisions planned or implemented in the system.
- Developers: Can provide technical details, if needed, during the analysis.

People from the following groups might also support an analysis:

- Operations or technical administration: People concerned with operating the system.
- Hardware: People concerned with the hardware the systems runs on. This is especially important for embedded systems.
- QA or testing: People working in quality assurance or testing of the system.
- Support: People working in support (first- or second level) of the system, who know about typical end-user issues.
- Users: People using or applying the system.

4.3.2 Exercises

P-question: Which two the following are *least likely* to support a qualitative analysis of your software architecture? Select *two* answers.

[ ]   Quality scenarios
[x]   Project budget report
[ ]   Architecture models
[ ]   Static source code metrics
[ ]   Performance metrics
[x]   Work breakdown structure

4.3.3 References

- [Clements+2002] is an extensive(!) introduction to systematic architecture evaluation and analysis.
- LG 4-1 introduces the term "quality" plus several other related terms.
- LG 4-2 shows how to clarify generic quality requirements and how to specify the generic terms for concrete systems.

LG 4-4: Quantitative evaluation

Quantitative evaluation of software architectures (R2)

Software architects know approaches for the quantitative analysis and evaluation (measurement) of software. They know that:

- Quantitative evaluation can help to identify critical parts within systems;
- Further information can be helpful for the evaluation of architectures, for example:
  - requirements and architecture documentation;
  - source code and related metrics such as lines of code, (cyclomatic) complexity, inbound and outbound dependencies;
  - known errors in source code, especially error clusters;
  - test cases and test results;
- The use of a metric as a target can lead to its invalidation (R2), as described, e.g., by Goodhart's law (R3).

4.4.1 Explanation

Quantitative evaluation (or -analysis) maps certain elements or aspects of a system to *numbers*.

Several metrics produce results specific to the programming language used. Comparing results between different languages is difficult if not impossible.

❗ Most often, metrics can only be indicators. They have to be regarded with appropriate context information.

There are a fair number of *metrics* available, plus (both free and commercial) tools to capture them.

Overview of (standard) software metrics

Metric	Description
Coupling	Degree of interdependence between building blocks of software; a measure of how closely connected two components are.
Cyclomatic complexity	Number of independent paths through a program's source code. For instance, if the source code contains no control flow statements, like conditionals or decisions, the cyclomatic complexity would be 1, since there is only a single path through the code. If the code has a single-condition IF statement, there would be two paths through the code: one where the IF statement evaluates to TRUE and another one where it evaluates to FALSE. In that case, the cyclomatic complexity would be 2. Two nested single-condition IFs, or one IF with two conditions, would produce a complexity of 4.
Lines of code	The simple size metric.
Test coverage	Degree to which the source code is tested by automatic tests.
Violation count (of rule <X>)	Number of violations against any given rule X, e.g. parameters need to be documented, method or function names should be longer than 3 letters etc.). Used to count violations against coding conventions or rules.

In addition to these simple metrics we propose to gather some additional quantitative information.

Overview of (standard) software metrics

Metric	Description
Bugs per component	How many bugs/issues do we have (current or historical) per component or subsystem? Here it's helpful to have an issue-tracking system in place which can keep track of the components or code artifacts ultimately responsible for the bug. The idea behind this metric is the Pareto principle: 20% of components contain 80% of the bugs.
Effort needed to fix bug in component	How much effort (in hours or days) is on average needed to ultimately fix a bug in a component? Might be differentiated for different bug categories to get more fine-grained results. Very helpful to locate time-to-market problems within software architectures.
Development effort per component	What fraction of the overall development effort (total, per year, per sprint or similar) is needed for this component? This often corresponds with "total amount spent for this component".
Developer sympathy per component	On a nominal scale, e.g. 1 (best) to 6 (worst), how much do developers like the component?

In practice it helps a great deal to correlate some of these non-standard metrics to the more conventional (e.g. coverage, complexity, coupling) to assist in identifying candidates for rework or refactoring.

! Avoid (or be at least very careful when) tying metrics to incentives or penalties for developers
● (e.g. can only commit code with a minimum percentage of comment lines). It may destroy the usefulness of that metric for obvious reasons.

4.4.2 Exercises

P-Question: Which metrics can help to predict errors or failures within your system?

Select the three most appropriate answers.

[ ] Tiobe index placement of the programming language used.
[x] Code complexity, like cyclomatic complexity or nesting level.
[x] Coupling.
[ ] Number of developers working on component.
[x] Number of bugs already known within component.

P-Question: You try to analyze your architecture quantitatively. Which are the two most appropriate indicators for architectural problem areas?

      [x] High coupling of components.
      [ ] Inappropriate names of public methods.
      [ ] Missing comments.
      [x] Error clusters.
      [ ] Number of test cases per component.

Reflect on the relation between metrics like "LoC" or complexity and the risk of runtime errors.

Reflect on useful combinations of two metrics ("two-dimensions").

For example:

- "How many errors occured in a certain subsystem" versus "What's the test-coverage in these subsystems"?
- "How often is a building-block (code artifact) changed" versus "What's the code complexity of this building-block"?

CPSA-F Chapter 5: Examples of software architectures

LG 5-1: From requirements to solutions

Know the relation between requirements, constraints, and solutions (R3)
Software architects are expected to recognize and comprehend the correlation between requirements and constraints, and the chosen solutions using at least one example.

5.1.1 Explanation

! This learning goal is not relevant for the examination.

You should have seen and understood the architecture of at least one system on a fairly detailed level. See the references below, especially [Starke+2019].

This learning goal proposes to watch for the relation between requirements and constraints on one hand and the solution decisions on the other. You should understand why the architects and/or the development team took certain decisions under the given constraints and requirements.

5.1.2 References

The following sources contain examples of software architectures together with quite detailed explanations:

- [Starke+2019] contains six detailed descriptions of real-world software systems. Available as Leanpub eBook and in print from Packt-Publishing.
- The collection "Architecture of Open Source Applications" (online:
  http://aosabook.org/en/index.html) describes numerous systems, although only a few on a detailed and technical level.

LG 5-2: Rationale of a technical implementation

Know the rationale of a solution's technical implementation (R3)
Software architects understand the technical realization (implementation, technical concepts, products used, architectural decisions, solution strategies) of at least one solution.

5.2.1 Explanation

! This learning goal is not relevant for the examination.

You should have seen and understood the major decisions and their reasons (aka: *rationale*) of at least one system on a fairly detailed level.

5.2.2 References

Please see [Starke+2019] and the references in LG 5-1.

Part III: Background

Content Overview
This part contains background information that is either required by multiple learning goals, is optional (R3), or otherwise deserves more in-depth treatment.

Additional patterns

Learning goal LG 2-5 covers some important architectural patterns with R1 examination relevance, but also contains a large number of optional "nice-to-know" patterns (R3).

We consider patterns to be a useful approach to software architecture, therefore we will introduce some *other* patterns mentioned in LG 2-5 with brief explanations.

! The following patterns are *not* relevant for the Foundation examination!

Adapter

Real-world adapter[32]

Decouple consumer and provider - where the interface of the provider does not exactly match that of the consumer. The adapter decouples one party from interface-changes in the other. The diagram shows a USB to micro-USB adapter.

Intent: Adapter makes otherwise incompatible elements cooperate.

Problem: An existing component offers some functionality that you would like to use, but its "view of the world" (its interface to the functionality) is not directly compatible with your system.

You need some way of *translating* or *adapting*.

---

32 Image created by https://www.flaticon.com/authors/freepik

Blackboard

The blackboard pattern is useful for systems that handle problems that cannot be solved by deterministic algorithms but require the combination of results from diverse knowledge sources, e.g. speech recognition.

Broker

This pattern is often to be found in distributed systems. A broker is responsible for coordinating communication between provider(s) and consumer(s). It handles forwarding requests and/or the transmission of results and exceptions.

Combinator (synonym: Closure of operations)

In functional programming, the combinator pattern is used to combine primitives into more complex structures: For domain object of type T, look for operations with both input and output type T. See [Yorgey2012].

Command

Intent: Command encapsulates everything needed to perform an action at a later time (create an object representing a method/function invocation). Command belongs to the *behavioral* patterns.

Application: Command has numerous real-life applications - here are some examples (some ideas quoted from Wikipedia, https://en.wikipedia.org/wiki/Command_pattern):

- **Macro recording**: If user actions are represented by command objects, a program can record a sequence of actions simply by keeping a list of the command objects as they are executed. It can then *play back* the same actions by executing the same command objects again in sequence.
- **Mobile code / networking**: It is possible to send whole command objects across the network to be executed on the other machines ("deliver behavior to remote locations").
- **Multi-level undo**: If user actions in a program are implemented as command objects, the program can keep a stack of the most recently executed commands. When the user wants to undo a command, the program simply pops the most recent command object and executes its undo() method.
- **Progress bars**: If a program executes a sequence of commands and needs to display the progress, and each command object has a `getEstimatedDuration()` method, the program can easily estimate the total duration.

CQRS (Command-Query-Responsibility-Segregation)

Separation of read-and-write concerns in information systems.
See https://martinfowler.com/bliki/CQRS.html

Event-sourcing

Handle operations on data by a sequence of events, each of which is recorded in an append-only store.

Facade

Simplifies the usage of a provider for consumer(s) by providing simplified access.

Intent: Facade provides a simpler interface to a complicated subsystem.

Problem: An existing subsystem is complicated or difficult to use. A consumer wants to access this subsystem, but does not want to use the complicated interface.

Solution: Create a "convenience interface" that facilitates access to the complex subsystem. Such a facade might require internal logic or processing.

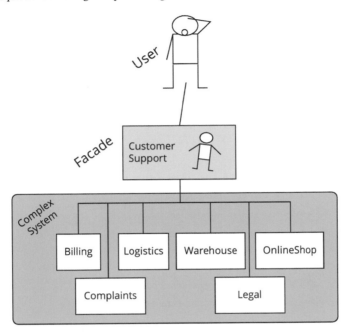

Real-world facade

Keep in mind: The facade pattern defines a new interface, whereas the adapter pattern uses an existing interface.

Integration and messaging patterns
A complete family of integration patterns has been created and described by [Hohpe+2003].

Interpreter
Represents a domain object or a DSL as syntax and provide functions implementing a semantic interpretation of the domain object(s) separately from the domain object itself.

MVC, MVVM, MV-update, PAC family of patterns
MVC and its variants separate presentation (view) from data, services and their coordination. Those patterns provide structures for (usually interactive) systems with a clear separation of concerns.

They are structured according to three major tasks:
- *Models contain core functionality and data.*
- *View components present views of the model, either to the user or in any other representation.*
- *Contro*llers accept user input and translate it to appropriate requests to the model and/or views. A change propagation mechanism takes care of propagation of changes to the model.

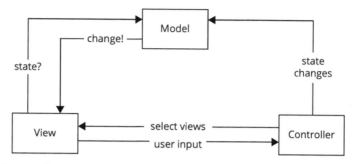

(Generic) Model-view-controller structure

Please note: The dependencies between model, view and controller might be slightly different in specific MVC frameworks (e.g. in web frameworks with communication over http).

Advantages:
- Multiple independent views of the same model;
- Views are synchronized with the model;
- Views can be dynamically attached (*plugged in*) at runtime;
- User interfaces (view) can be modified without changing the model.

Disadvantages:
- Quite complex for simple systems;
- Frequent events may overload the change propagation mechanism;
- Changes to the model might become expensive if many views are involved.

Observer
A producer of values over time notifies a central switch board where consumers can register to be notified of changes.

Plug-In
Extends the behavior of a component.

Ports&Adapters
Concentrate domain logic in the center of the system, have connections to the outside world (database, UI) at the edges. The direction of dependencies is only outside-in, never inside-out.

(Synonyms: Onion-Architecture, Hexagonal-Architecture)

Personal comment from Gernot: In my opinion, this is the most useful and important of all patterns. It's the foundation of *domain-driven-design* done-right, and provides the perfect separation of technology and business/domain logic.

Proxy

An intermediate between consumer and provider, enabling temporal decoupling, caching of results, controlling access to the provider etc. The proxy can control access to the real subject, can cache results or defer calls. No change is needed on the consumer and the real subject.

Intent: A proxy represents another element, provides a surrogate or placeholder for another element, e.g. to control access or add functionality to it.

Problem: Some elements (in the figure below it's called `RealSubject`) might be resource-intensive, overloaded or difficult to enhance.

Solution: The proxy (placeholder) provides exactly the same interface as the original object. In the following figure it's called `doSomething()`. A Consumer needing `doSomething()` gets a reference to the `Proxy` instead of the `RealSubject`.

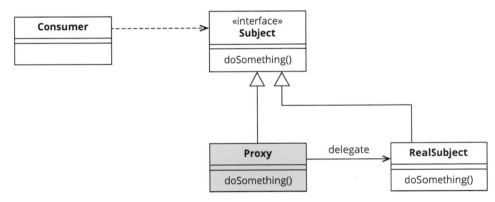

Proxy

Common applications:

- Security (or protection) proxy: can be used to control access to a resource.
- Remote proxy: In distributed (object) programming, a local object (*proxy*) represents a remote object (one that lives in a different address space).
- Virtual proxy: If some resource is *expensive* in terms of memory, capacity, computing power or similar, a proxy (skeleton) implementation might be helpful sometimes.
- Caching proxy: Stores results that have already been computed by the original object.

Distinction: Adapter provides a different interface to its subject. Proxy provides the same interface.

Remote procedure call

Make a function or algorithm execute in a different address space.

SOA

Service-oriented architecture. An approach to provide abstract services rather than concrete implementations to users of the system in order to promote reuse of services across departments and between companies.

Template and strategy

Make specific algorithms flexible by encapsulating them.

Visitor

Separate data-structure traversal from specific processing.

References

- The Sourcemaking site is a readable and friendly introduction to (design) patterns: https://sourcemaking.com/design_patterns.

Appropriateness: it always depends. . .

Strive for → appropriateness. In your role as software architect you (and your team) have to take numerous *meta decisions*, that do not directly influence the implementation, the internal structure or concepts of your system. Here are just a few examples of these:
- The effort you invest in each of the six tasks (see LG 1-4);
- Whether to apply proven technologies or try out innovative approaches;
- The amount of detail you put into written documentation;
- The level of formalism you apply to your documentation;
- The time you spend with specific stakeholders;
- The order in which you tackle your tasks and activities;
- The amount of discussion time you allocate for a specific design decision;
- The kind of feedback you gather from various stakeholders.

All these things cannot be decided *in general*, but have to be decided depending on your current situation. All these need to be done *adequately*.

It depends on. . . (for example)
- Risk: The more risk in your project/system, the more quality assurance effort you are likely to invest. Maybe even more formalism or documentation. . .
- Complexity: The more business or technical complexity exists in your project/system, the more effort you spend on reducing complexity or making it accessible, e.g. by coaching or documentation.
- Budget or time: If either budget or time are severely limited, you will likely reduce documentation, formalism or other activities that are not immediately related to project success. Maybe that will create technical debt and haunt you in the future, but today you don't care.
- Team: With an awesome and experienced team, you might reduce communication and documentation to a bare minimum. On the other hand, unexperienced team members might require excessive communication and coaching effort.
- Formal regulations: If your organization is regulated by law or other kinds of formal contracts, you will invest effort in documentation and formalism to satisfy these kinds of constraints.
- Critical quality requirements: Examples might include "ultra-high security" or "life critical safety" applications where you'll work hard to fix *every* loose end, try every kind of feedback or test available, do formal reviews and inspections and so forth.

Part IV: Moving on

This section outlines advanced topics that will likely be both valuable and interesting for your professional career in software architecture.

> **Content overview**
> - Overview of advanced topics (*modules*) in software architecture education;
> - CPSA-Advanced Level Certification.

Advanced Level modules

Below you will find an overview of the Advanced Level modules (as of April 2023).

Short	Name
ADOC	Architecture documentation
AGILA	Agile software architecture
ARCEVAL	Architecture evaluation
BLOCKCHAIN	Low-trust consensus in decentralized applications
CLOUDINFRA	Infrastructure, container and cloud native
DDD	Domain-driven design
EAM	Enterprise architecture management
EMBEDDED	Embedded systems
FLEX	Flexible architectural models
FUNAR	Functional software architecture
IMPROVE	Evolution and improvement of software architectures
REQ4ARC	Requirements for software architects
SOFT	Soft skills for software architects
WEB	Web architecture
WEBSEC	Web security

ADOC: Architecture documentation

How to document and communicate software architectures?

ADOC provides the skills to:
- Document software architectures;
- Evaluate existing documentation with regard to its suitability and adequacy;
- Improve existing documentation.

Participants learn to systematically describe the essential aspects of software architectures (including decisions, structures, concepts, quality requirements and views). For this purpose, ADOC explains fundamental notations and documentation methods. It shows examples of various tools for the practical implementation of architecture documentation.

AGILA: Agile software architecture

How to accomplish effective architecture work in Agile teams and projects?

Participants learn how to design, develop and further develop software systems and architectures in accordance with Agile principles. The module covers the application of Agile principles and concepts to architecture work. It teaches anchoring of fundamental architecture practices in an Agile approach.

ARCEVAL: Architecture evaluation

How to determine whether architecture meets expectations?

Participants learn how to methodically analyze and evaluate software architecture with a focus on qualitative analysis.

BLOCKCHAIN: Low-trust consensus in decentralized applications

How to leverage blockchain technologies to establish consensus in distributed, low-trust systems?

The term *blockchain* describes a set of heterogeneous technologies for designing distributed systems that are able to establish consensus about stored data and procedures. Pioneered as a system to allow transfer of secure monetary tokens, blockchains have since evolved to application platforms for executing smart contracts written in domain-specific languages. The central idea, common to all blockchain implementations, is that transactions can be stored in an append-only ledger that is maintained on multiple nodes, thus increasing resiliency and decreasing the potential for fraudulent modifications.

Participants of this module will gain a deep understanding of various flavors of blockchain technologies, platform requirements and abilities, including languages for smart contracts.

CLOUDINFRA: Infrastructure, container and cloud native

How to design and implement adjustable infrastructure for the cloud?

Microservices, containers and container managers have considerably changed the way in which we design, develop and deploy software in recent years. Modern applications must work in a cluster of several nodes, be dynamically scalable and fault-tolerant. Participants will learn ways to implement dynamic cloud-native architectures, container application design, logging/monitoring/alerting, container native storage and options for UI integration. Typical concepts of current container managers will also be demonstrated.

DDD: Domain-driven design

How to design domain-centered architecture in cooperation with business experts and developers?

Participants will become familiar with the principles of domain-driven design and will be able to apply them to the design and implementation of software systems. With the help of the communication skills taught, they will be able to establish a uniform language between business experts and developers.

EAM: Enterprise architecture management
How to maintain consistency within a large IT system and application landscape?

Participants learn about terms, methods and procedures used in enterprise architecture management. They will get to know about IT governance and approaches for implementing EAM with EA-frameworks.

EMBEDDED: Embedded systems
How to design embedded systems that have a direct impact on their environments?

This module concentrates on software development and architecture design for embedded systems, with a strong focus on functional safety aspects.

FLEX: Flexible architectural models
How to develop the most flexible architectures?

Participants learn how to optimize software architectures for rapid deployment. Microservices and self-contained systems are core topics. They will learn how to combine domain-oriented modularization principles with modern infrastructure approaches.

FUNAR: Functional software architecture
How to design architecture with functions, immutable data and combinators?

The module presents functional software architecture as an alternative to object-oriented architecture.

Compared to OO architecture, functional software architecture relies on immutable data, algebraic abstractions and embedded domain-specific languages. The results are flexible and robust architectures that are less complex and have fewer hidden dependencies than OO.

Participants will know the essential principles of functional architecture and will be able to apply them when designing software systems. They will know the peculiarities of functional programming languages and can use them effectively when implementing software systems.

IMPROVE: Evolution and improvement of software architectures
How to improve software systems, focused on economic and technical objectives?

Participants will learn how to systematically improve existing (*legacy*) systems. The module explains methodical improvement based upon three iterative phases:

- Systematically analyze the existing problems in systems and associated processes;
- Evaluate or prioritize these problems, to avoid solving *trivial* problems;
- The actual *improvement* itself.

 (personal opinion from Gernot) In IT education, the main focus lies on constructing systems *from scratch*. In reality, though, about 75% of development time is spent maintaining existing systems. This module teaches how to do deal with legacy systems, and how to systematically improve them.

REQ4ARC: Requirements for software architects

How to equip development teams with enough requirements engineering know-how, so they can base their decisions on the real needs of stakeholders?

Software architects will learn about professional requirements engineering. They will acquire a basic knowledge in requirements elicitation and management to help in developing the right products.

Key topics discussed include product goals versus project goals, scoping and context definition, functional and quality requirements, behavior-driven development and requirements prioritization. In addition, options for the effective integration of requirements-analysis and -management into development processes are discussed.

 (personal opinion from Gernot) Getting the *requirements right* belongs to the most underrated architecture activities, although it can dramatically improve the efficiency and effectiveness of development teams. This module teaches everything you need to get better requirements!

SOFT: Soft skills for software architects

How can software architects lead and moderate discussions on architecture determination and present their architecture in a comprehensible manner?

Participants are introduced to the fundamentals of communication models and types, acquire techniques and skills for one-on-one and group discussions, as well as visualization and moderation techniques. Further topics include the fundamentals of conflict management and reflection techniques.

WEB: Web architecture

How to design effective and secure web-based systems?

This module starts with an introduction to basic concepts from the web environment, protocols and standards. Architectural styles for the web, especially REST, stateful backend web apps, single-page applications and web components will be introduced. These topics are complemented by the transfer of knowledge about the necessary technologies and infrastructure solutions.

The focus is on the design of web architectures and techniques for identifying and achieving quality attributes such as security, scalability, availability, operability and accessibility.

WEBSEC: Web security

How to achieve and improve security in web-based systems?

Software architects learn what "security" is and how it can be integrated into their own analysis and development processes. The technical focus is on web-based systems. Topics included in the curriculum are, for example, secure design and development processes, cryptography, possible attack vectors as well as security and infrastructure.

Advanced Level certification

To quote from the iSAQB Advanced Level website:

"As a follow-on to the Foundation Level, which has been available for some time now, iSAQB's Advanced Level is the next logical step in qualifying software architecture professionals. Developed according to iSAQB's specification, this training scheme follows a modular structure and requires successful trainees to demonstrate comprehensive knowledge and skills."

To successfully practice as an (advanced) software architect, people generally need skills and experience in the following four skill areas:

- **Domain** (or business), the subject area of the systems you're working on.
- **Methodical** skills, systematic approaches to architectural tasks, independent of technologies and organization.
- **Technological** skills, knowledge and implementation of technology solutions used in design tasks.
- **Communicative** skills, like presentation, argumentation, communication and moderation skills as well as the ability to cooperate productively with different stakeholders.

The iSAQB publishes various curriculum modules covering the latter three of these areas (methodical, technical, and communication skills). These training modules are offered by numerous training providers and organizations - they have to be licensed by iSAQB and will be subject to formal audits by iSAQB to ensure a high and consistent quality of the trainings.

Candidates for the CPSA-Advanced can choose their own desired path through these learning modules.

Prerequisites for Advanced Level certification

To successfully master the CPSA-Advanced Level certification, candidates need the following prerequisites:

- iSAQB CPSA-Foundation Level examination.
- A minimum of three years' full-time professional experience in the IT industry, working on design and development of at least two different IT systems.
- At least 70 credit points (CPs) in iSAQB licensed advanced level trainings, with at least 10 CPs in each of the three skill areas (methodical, technical, communicative).
- A written nondisclosure agreement covering the examination task and its solution.

Advanced Level certification

Achieving the CPSA-Advanced Level certification requires several steps:

1. Candidates need to fulfill all prerequisites (see above).
2. Candidates need to attend licensed Advanced Level trainings to acquire appropriate skills. Each training yields 20-30 credit points.
   - At least 70 credit points are required;

- It's possible to participate in Advanced Level trainings without having all CPSA-Advanced prerequisites.
3. The certification body will issue an *examination task*, describing a hypothetical situation where an architectural solution for an IT system is required.
4. Candidates are required to provide a written (up to 40 pages) solution to this problem. They may take up to six month to complete the task. Creating this solution will typically require at least 40 hours of work.
5. Two independent examiners (appointed by the iSAQB and the certification body) will anonymously review this solution. During review, the identity of the candidate is not revealed to the examiners. If both examiners rate the solution as sufficient, the candidate is allowed to proceed to the final step of the CPSA-Advanced certification, the interview.
6. In the final stage, the candidate needs to conduct an interview with the two examiners for approximately 30-60 minutes. If both examiners rate the interview as sufficient, the candidate passes the CPSA-Advanced Level examination and will receive a CPSA-A certification.

 Most candidates need more than the designated 40 hours to complete the written examination. We propose that you should take a week off your normal job and tackle the Advanced-exam in one single go. That will save you a lot of time, as you won't suffer from many mental context switches.

Part V: Appendices

Content overview

A. Background info on the authors.
B. Glossary of terms. Some of these are referenced in the iSAQB curriculum [iSAQB-FLC] and might be important for the examination.
C. References. A collection of resources and references, with some personal comments.

Appendix A: About the authors

Dr. Gernot Starke (INNOQ Fellow) is co-founder and longstanding user of the (open source) arc42 documentation template. For more than 20 years he has worked as a software architect, coach and consultant, conquering the challenges of creating effective software architectures for clients from various industries.

In 2008 Gernot co-founded the International Software Architecture Qualification Board (iSAQB e.V.) and since then has supported it as an active member. As a licensed trainer he has conducted public and in-house workshops and training classes for more than 2,000 individuals. In 2014 he founded the (open source) Architecture Improvement Method aim42. Gernot has authored several (German) books on software architecture, patterns and related topics. Find more on his website (https://gernotstarke.de).

Gernot studied computer science at the Institute of Technology in Aachen (RWTH Aachen). He then worked as a developer and consultant for smaller software companies, before returning to university to undertake international research on methodical software engineering. In 1995 he received his PhD from Johannes Kepler University of Linz, Austria (Prof. Gerhard Chroust) for his thesis on "Software Process Modeling". He then joined Schumann AG in Cologne and was involved in consulting and development work for several years.

He became technical director of the "Object Reality Center", a joint venture with Sun Microsystems and led the first European Java Project (for Hypobank in Munich). Since then he has consulted and coached numerous clients from various domains, mainly finance, insurance, telecommunication, logistics, automotive and industry on topics around software engineering, software development and development process organization. He has (co-)architected and helped to implement numerous information systems in various industries.

Parallel to his architecture work and coaching/training, he conducts reviews and/or audits, helping clients identify opportunities for improvement within systems and their development processes. Gernot has served the Foundation Level working group since 2008 and took over the chair of this group in 2015.

He lives in Cologne with his wife (*Cheffe Uli*) and is proud father of two (grown-up) kids.

Dr.-Ing. Alexander Lorz is a freelance software architecture trainer, IT consultant and developer. His first contact with IT systems dates back to the mid-1980s, and since then he has refused to give up his fascination for the science and craftsmanship of developing complex systems.

Alexander studied computer science at the Dresden University of Technology and worked as a researcher, educator and PhD student at the Heinz-Nixdorf Endowed Chair for Multimedia Technology. During this time he participated in a wide range of academic research and industry-founded projects, e.g. on improving cooperation and job satisfaction in virtual teams and corporations, and on end user-driven composition of applications and user interfaces. In 2010 he received his PhD on the topic of adaptable and adaptive questionnaires under the mentorship of Prof. Dr.-Ing. Klaus Meißner.

After working as research group coordinator, he joined the Dresden-based intecsoft group as a software architect, developer and technical project manager. Projects he contributed to were located in the fields of electromobility, document and transaction processing as well as digitalization of business processes. Since 2016 he has been working as a coach and trainer in software architecture for a large number of course participants from various sectors, e.g. automotive suppliers, fintech companies, public authorities, automation technology, telecommunications and IT service providers.

He lives with his family in Dresden and is an enthusiastic member of the regional maker scene.

Appendix B: Glossary of terms

 This glossary contains only the most important terms which might appear in the iSAQB examination. The official (and free!) iSAQB Glossary of Software Architecture Terminology[33] is more comprehensive and will surely be helpful, especially if you're interested in additional iSAQB documents, for example the CPSA-Advanced curriculae. This glossary is curated in synchronization with the iSAQB glossary, i.e. additions to one document are entered into the other whenever they are relevant. The iSAQB glossary is licensed under a Creative Commons Attribution 4.0 International License[34].

 Personal comment
Some terms within this glossary contain personal comments or opinions.

Abstraction
The process of removing details to focus attention on aspects of greater importance. Similar in nature to the process of generalization.

A view of an element that focuses on the information relevant to a particular purpose, ignoring additional or other information.

A design construct as in "Building blocks should depend on abstractions rather than on implementations."

Abstractness
Metric for the source code of object-oriented systems: The number of abstract types (interfaces and abstract classes) divided by the total number of types.

Adapter
The adapter is a design pattern that allows the interface of an existing component to be used from another interface. It is often used to make existing components cooperate with others without modifying their source code. For details, see Part III on the adapter pattern.

Aggregation
A form of object composition in object-oriented programming.

It differs from → composition, as aggregation does not imply ownership. When the element is destroyed, the contained elements remain intact.

---

33 https://public.isaqb.org/glossary/
34 https://creativecommons.org/licenses/by/4.0/

Appropriateness

It depends. (syn: adequacy, suitability) Suitability for a particular purpose. See "It depends"

 Personal comment (Gernot)
"It depends" is a fundamentally useful heuristic in software architecture, as there is no silver bullet or no single recipe for all circumstances. Adjust your decisions according to risk, complexity, team, time, budget, technology, organization, context or other factors - and don't believe the crowd or blindly follow the hype.

arc42

Free arc42 template for communication and documentation of software architectures.

Although highly pragmatic and grounded in massive practical experience from various domains, arc42 is not relevant for the iSAQB examination.

Find the documentation on docs.arc42.org.

Architecture

See →software architecture.

Architectural decision

Decision, which has a sustainable or essential effect on the architecture of a system.

Example: Decision about database technology or technical basics of the user interface.

Following ISO/IEC/IEEE 42010, an architectural decision pertains to system concerns. However, there is often no simple mapping between the two. A decision can affect the architecture in several ways. These can be reflected in the architecture description (as defined in ISO/IEC/IEEE 42010).

Architecture description

Work product used to express an architecture (as defined in ISO/IEC/IEEE 42010).

Architecture evaluation

Determine if an architecture can achieve its target qualities or quality attributes.

Quantitative or qualitative assessment of a (software or system) architecture.

In our opinion the term *architecture analysis* would more appropriate, as *evaluation* contains *value*, implying numerical assessment (which is usually only part of what you should do in architecture analysis).

Architecture goal

(syn: Architectural quality goal, Architectural quality requirement): A quality attribute that the system needs to achieve, where that quality attribute is understood to be an architectural issue.

Hence, the architecture needs to be designed in a way to fulfill this architectural goal. These goals often have *long term character* in contrast to (short term) project goals.

Architecture model

An architecture view is composed of one or more architecture models. An architecture model uses modelling conventions appropriate to the concerns to be addressed. These conventions are specified by the model kind governing that model. Within an architecture description, an architecture model can be a part of more than one architecture view (as defined in ISO/IEC/IEEE 42010).

Architecture objective

See → architecture goal.

Architectural (architecture) pattern

"An architectural pattern expresses a fundamental structural organization scheme for software systems. It provides a set of predefined subsystems, specifies their responsibilities, and includes rules and guidelines for organizing the relationships between them" ([Buschmann+1996], page 12). Similar to → architecture style.

Architecture style

Description of element and relation types, together with constraints on how they can be used. Often called → architecture pattern. Examples: pipes-and-filters, model-view-controller, layers.

 Personal comment (Alexander)

Depending on who you ask, some might consider architecture styles a generalization of architecture patterns. That is, "distributed system" is a style while "client-server, CQRS, broker and peer-to-peer" are more specific patterns that belong to this style. However, from a practical point of view this distinction is not essential.

Architectural tactic

A technique, strategy, approach or decision helping to achieve one or several quality requirements. The term was coined by [Bass+2021].

Architectural view

A representation of a system from a specific perspective. Important and well-known views are:
- → context view;
- → building block view;
- → runtime view;
- → deployment view.

You can find brief examples in sections LG 3-5 and LG 3-6. [Bass+2021] and [Rozanski+11] discuss this concept extensively.

Artifact

Tangible by-product created or generated during development of software. Examples of artifacts are use cases, all kinds of diagrams, UML models, requirements and design documents, source code, test cases, class-files and archives.

Association

Defines a relationship between objects (in general: between modules or components). Each association can be described in detail by cardinalities and (role-)names.

See → coupling, → dependency, and → relationship.

ATAM

Architecture Tradeoff Analysis Method. Qualitative architecture evaluation method, based upon a (hierarchical) quality tree and concrete quality scenarios.

Basic idea: Compare fine-grained quality scenarios ("quality-requirements") with the corresponding architectural approaches to identify risks, non-risks, trade-offs and sensitivity points.

Black box (often written *blackbox*)

View of a building block (or component) that hides the internal structure. Black boxes respect the → information hiding principle. They shall have clearly defined input and output interfaces plus a precisely formulated *responsibility* or *objective*. Optionally a black box defines some quality attributes, for example timing behavior, throughput or security aspects.

Bottom-up approach

Direction of work (or strategy of processing) or modeling and design. Starting with something detailed or concrete, working towards something more general or abstract.

"In a bottom-up approach, the individual base elements of the system are first specified in great detail. These elements are then linked together to form larger subsystems." (quote from Wikipedia, https://en.wikipedia.org/wiki/Top-down_and_bottom-up_design)

Bridge

Design pattern in which an abstraction is decoupled from its implementation, so that the two can vary independently. In case you find that incomprehensible (as most people do) - have a look at http://www.cs.sjsu.edu/~pearce/modules/patterns/platform/bridge/index.htm

Broker

An architecture pattern used to structure distributed software systems with decoupled components that interact by (usually remote) service invocations.

A broker is responsible for coordinating communication, such as forwarding requests, as well as for transmitting results and exceptions.

Building block

General or abstract term for all kinds of artifacts from which software is constructed. Part of the statical structure → building block view) of software architecture. Building blocks can be hierarchically structured - they may contain other (smaller) building blocks.

Examples: Component, module, package, namespace, class, file, program, subsystem, configuration, data-definition etc.

Building block view

Shows the statical structure of the system, how its source code is organized.

The building block view is usually organized in a hierarchy, starting from the → context view. Usually it is complemented by one or several runtime scenarios in the → runtime view.

Business architecture

A blueprint of an enterprise providing a common understanding of the organization. It is used to align strategic objectives and tactical demands.

C4 Model

The C4 Model for Software Architecture Documentation [Brown-C4] was developed by Simon Brown. It consists of a hierarchical set of software architecture diagrams for context, containers, components and code. The hierarchy of the C4 diagrams provides different levels of abstraction, each of which is relevant to a different audience.

Cohesion

The degree to which elements of a building block, component or module belong together is called cohesion. It measures the strength of the relationship between pieces of functionality within a given component. In cohesive systems, functionality is strongly related. It is usually characterized as *high cohesion* or *low cohesion*.

Strive for high cohesion, because high cohesion often implies reusability, low coupling and better understandability.

Command

Design pattern in which an object is used to encapsulate an action. This action might be invoked or executed at a later time.

Complexity

"Complexity is generally used to characterize something with many parts where those parts interact with each other in multiple ways."

(quoted from Wikipedia, see https://en.wikipedia.org/wiki/Complexity.)

- *"Essential* complexity is the core of the problem we have to solve, and it consists of the parts of the software that are legitimately difficult problems. Most software problems contain some complexity.
- *Accidental* complexity is all the stuff that doesn't necessarily relate directly to the solution, but that we have to deal with anyway." (quoted from Mark Needham[35])

Architects should strive to reduce accidental complexity.

Component

See → building block. Structural element of an architecture.

Composition

Combines simpler elements (e.g. functions, data types, building blocks) to build more complicated, powerful or more responsible ones. In UML: When the owning element is destroyed, so are the contained elements.

Concept

Plan, principle(s) or rule(s) on how to solve a specific problem. Concepts are often *cross-cutting* in a sense that multiple architectural elements might be affected by a single concept. That means that implementors of e.g. implementation units (building blocks) should adhere to the corresponding concept. Concepts form the basis for *conceptual integrity* (see below).

Conceptual integrity

Concepts, rules, patterns and similar solution approaches are applied in a consistent (homogeneous, similar) way throughout the system. Similar problems are solved in similar or identical ways.

 Personal comment

Maybe the single most important factor influencing maintainability of medium to large systems, strong positive correlation to understandability. Downside: Sometimes adherence to "given rules" hinders *innovation*.

Concern

"A *concern* about an architecture is a requirement, an objective, a constraint, an intention, or an aspiration a stakeholder has for that architecture." (quoted from [Rozanski+11], chapter 8)

Following ISO/IEC/IEEE 42010 a concern is defined as (system) interest in a system relevant to one or more of its stakeholders (as defined in ISO/IEC/IEEE 42010).

---

35 https://www.markhneedham.com/blog/2010/03/18/essential-and-accidental-complexity/

Please note: A concern pertains to any influence on a system in its environment, including developmental, technological, business, operational, organizational, political, economic, legal, regulatory, ecological and social influences.

Consistency

A consistent system does not contain contradictions. Some examples of consistency:

- Identical problems are solved by identical (or at least similar) approaches.
- Degree to which data and their relations comply with validation rules.
- Clients (of a database) get identical results for identical queries (e.g. Monotonic-Read-Consistency, Monotonic-Write-Consistency, Read-Your-Writes-Consistency etc.).

With respect to behavior: Degree, to which a system behaves in a coherent, replicable and reasonable way.

Constraint

A restriction on the degree of freedom you have in creating, designing, implementing or otherwise providing a solution. Constraints are often *global requirements*, such as limited development resources or a decision by senior management that restricts the way you plan, design, develop or operate a system.

Based upon a definition from Scott Ambler on http://agilemodeling.com/artifacts/constraint.htm

Context (of a system)

"Defines the relationships, dependencies, and interactions between the system and its environment: People, systems, and external entities with which it interacts." (quoted from [Rozanski+11], see also this excerpt[36])

Another definition from arc42: "System scope and context - as the name suggests - delimits your system (i.e. your scope) from all its communication partners (neighboring systems and users, i.e. the context of your system). It thereby specifies the external interfaces." (quoted from [arc42] docs)

Distinguish between *business* and *technical* context:

The **business** context (formerly called *logical* context) shows the external relationships from a business- or non-technical perspective. It abstracts from technical, hardware or implementation details. Input/output relationships are named by their *business meaning* instead of their technical properties.

The **technical** context shows technical details, like transmission channel, technical protocol, IP-address, bus or similar hardware details.

---

36 https://www.viewpoints-and-perspectives.info/home/viewpoints/context/

Embedded systems, for example, often care for hardware-related information very early in development.

Context view

Shows the complete system as one black box within its environment, either from a business perspective (*business context*) or from a technical or deployment perspective (*technical context*). The context view (or context diagram) shows the boundary between a system and its environment, showing the entities in its environment (its neighbors) with which it interacts.

Neighbors can either be other software systems, hardware (like sensors), humans, user-roles or even organizations using the system.

See → context.

Coupling

Coupling[37] is the kind and degree of *interdependence* between building blocks of software, a measure of how closely connected two components are.

You should always aim for *low* coupling.

Coupling is usually contrasted with → cohesion. Low coupling often correlates with high cohesion, and vice versa. Low coupling is often a sign of a well-structured system. When combined with high cohesion, it supports understandability and maintainability.

CQRS

(command query responsibility segregation): Separate the elements manipulating (*command*) data from those just reading (*query*). This separation enables different optimization strategies for reading and writing data.

For example, it's much easier to cache data that's read-only than to cache data that's also altered.

There's an interesting eBook by Mark Nijhof[38] on this subject.

Cross-cutting concept

See → concept.

Cross-cutting concern

Functionality of the architecture or system that affects several elements. Examples of such concerns are logging, transactions, security, exception handling, caching etc.

---

37 https://en.wikipedia.org/wiki/Coupling_(computer_programming)
38 https://leanpub.com/cqrs

Often these concerns will be addressed in systems via → concepts.

Curriculum

The learning process provided by a school, here: iSAQB as the institution governing software architecture education. It includes the content of courses (the syllabus), the methods employed and other aspects, like norms and values, which relate to the way the education, including certification and examination, is organized.

Cyclomatic complexity

Quantitative measure of the number of independent paths through a program's source code. It roughly correlates to the number of conditional statements (`if`, `while`) in the code +1. A linear sequence of statements without "`if`" or "`while`" has the cyclomatic complexity of 1. Many software engineers believe that higher complexity correlates to the number of defects.

Decomposition

(syn: *factoring*) Breaking or dividing a complex system or problem into several smaller parts that are easier to understand, implement or maintain.

Dependency

See → coupling.

Dependency Injection (DI)

Instead of having your objects or a factory creating a dependency, you pass the needed dependencies to the constructor or provide property setters. You therefore make the creation of specific dependencies *somebody else's problem.*

Dependency inversion principle

One of the SOLID principles, nicely explained by Brett Schuchert[39]. High level elements should not depend upon low level elements.

Consumers should not depend on concrete providers, but on an abstraction of the provider. In OO programming, it's often implemented by interface inheritance: A consumer depends upon an interface.

The concrete implementation of that interface is determined (and/or injected) at runtime.

See also → dependency injection.

Deployment

Bring software into its execution environment (hardware, processor etc.). Put software into operation.

---

39 https://martinfowler.com/articles/dipInTheWild.html

Deployment view

Architectural view showing the technical infrastructure where a system or artifacts will be deployed and executed.

"This view defines the physical environment in which the system is intended to run, including the hardware environment your system needs (e.g., processing nodes, network interconnections, and disk storage facilities), the technical environment requirements for each node (or node type) in the system, and the mapping of your software elements to the runtime environment that will execute them." (as defined by [Rozanski+11], see also this excerpt).

Design pattern

General or generic reusable solution to a commonly occurring problem within a given context in design.

Initially conceived by the famous architect Christopher Alexander, the concept of *design patterns* was taken up by software engineers. In our opinion, every serious software developer should know the pioneering Gang-of-Four[40] book [Gamma+1995] by Erich Gamma and his three allies.

Design principle

Set of guidelines that helps software developers to design and implement better solutions, where "better" could, for example, mean one or more of the following:

- Low → coupling;
- High → cohesion;
- → Separation of concerns or adherence to the → single responsibility principle;
- Adherence to the → information hiding principle;
- Avoid *Rigidity*: A system or element is difficult to change because every change potentially affects many other elements;
- Avoid *Fragility*: When elements are changed, unexpected results, defects or otherwise negative consequences occur at other elements;
- Avoid *Immobility*: An element is difficult to reuse because it cannot be disentangled from the rest of the system.

Design rationale

An explicit documentation of the reasons behind decisions made when designing any architectural element.

Domain-driven design (DDD)

"Domain-driven design (DDD) is an approach to developing software for complex needs by deeply connecting the implementation to an evolving model of the core business concepts." (quoted from DDDCommunity[41]). See [Evans-2003].

---

40 https://en.wikipedia.org/wiki/Design_Patterns
41 https://dddcommunity.org/learning-ddd/what_is_ddd/

Domain model

The domain model is a concept of → domain-driven design. It provides a system of abstractions that describes selected aspects of a domain and can be used to solve problems related to that domain.

Embedded system

System *embedded* within a larger mechanical or electrical system. Embedded systems often have real-time computing constraints. Typical properties of embedded systems are low power consumption, limited memory and processing resources, small size and intermittent or non-existent network connectivity.

Encapsulation

Encapsulation has two slightly distinct notions, and sometimes can be the combination thereof:
• Restricting access to some of the object's components;
• Bundling of data with the methods or functions operating on that data.

Encapsulation is a mechanism for → information hiding.

Enterprise IT architecture

Synonym: Enterprise architecture.

Structures and concepts for the IT support of an entire company. Atomic subject matters of the enterprise architecture are single software systems also referred to as "applications".

Environment

(System) context determining the setting and circumstances of all influences upon a system (as defined in ISO/IEC/IEEE 42010).

Please note: The environment of a system includes developmental, technological, business, operational, organizational, political, economic, legal, regulatory, ecological and social influences.

Facade

(Design pattern) A Facade offers a simplified interface to a complex or complicated building block (the *provider*) without any modifications to the provider.

For details, see Part III on the facade pattern.

Factory

(Design pattern) In class-based or object-oriented programming, the factory (method) pattern is a creational design pattern that uses factory methods or factory components for creating objects, without having to specify the exact class of the object that will be created.

In general, a *factory* is a building block to construct (usually instances) of other building blocks *at runtime*.

Fallacies of distributed computing

The fallacies of distributed computing were originally postulated by Peter L. Deutsch and contain seven statements, which are *wrong assumptions* taken by people inexperienced in distributed computing. See the Wikipedia page[42] on this. In brief, the seven fallacies are:

- The network is reliable;
- Latency is zero;
- Bandwidth is infinite;
- The network is secure;
- Topology doesn't change;
- There is one administrator;
- Transport cost is zero.

Filter

Part of the pipes-and-filters architectural style that creates or transforms data. Filters are typically executed independently from other filters.

Fitness function

"An architectural fitness function provides an objective integrity assessment of some architectural characteristics." [Ford+2017]. A fitness function is derived from manual evaluations and automated tests and shows to what extent architectural or quality requirements are met.

Function signature

(Synonym: type or method signature) Defines input and output of functions or methods.

A signature can include:

- parameters and their types;
- return value and type;
- exceptions thrown or errors raised.

Fundamental Modeling Concepts (FMC)

Fundamental Modeling Concepts [Wendt-FMC] is a graphical notation for modeling and documenting software systems. From their website:

"FMC provides a framework for the comprehensive description of software-intensive systems. It is based on a precise terminology and supported by a graphical notation which can be easily understood".

Personal comment
Although well suited for describing statical and dynamical structures of (software) systems, it has not found its way out of purely academical context. In my opinion, it is of limited practical relevance.

---

42 https://en.wikipedia.org/wiki/Fallacies_of_distributed_computing

Gateway

(Design or architecture pattern): An element that encapsulates access to a (usually external) system or resource.

See → wrapper, → adapter.

Global analysis

Systematic approach to achieve desired quality attributes.

Developed and documented by Christine Hofmeister (Siemens Corporate Research), explained in their (out-of-print) book [Hofmeister+1999].

Heterogeneous architectural style

See → hybrid architecture style.

Heuristic

Informal rule, rule-of-thumb. Any way of problem-solving not guaranteed to be optimal, but somehow sufficient.

Examples from Object-Oriented Design[43] or User Interface Design[44].

Hybrid architecture style

Combination of two or more existing architecture styles or patterns.

For example, an MVC construct embedded in a layer structure, with a pipes-and-filters structure within the model of the MVC.

IEEE1471

Standard *Recommended Practice for Architectural Description of Software-Intensive Systems*, redefined as ISO/IEC 42010:2007.

Defines an (abstract) framework for the description of software architectures.

Incremental development

See → iterative and incremental development.

Information hiding

A fundamental principle in software design: Keep those design or implementation decisions *hidden* that are likely to change, thus protecting other parts of the system from modification if these decisions or implementations are changed.

---

43 http://www.vincehuston.org/ood/oo_design_heuristics.html
44 https://www.nngroup.com/articles/ten-usability-heuristics/

Information hiding is one important property of → black boxes.

The term → encapsulation is often used interchangeably with information hiding.

Interface

Multiple meanings, depending on context:
1. Shared boundary across which two building blocks interact or communicate with each other.
2. Design construct that provides an abstraction of the behavior of concrete components, and declares possible interactions with these components and constraints for these interactions. In that sense, an interface is "light-weight inheritance".

An interface in the sense of the first meaning (*interaction*) could, for example, be used for a method or function invocation, message passing, notification, data transfer or other kinds of synchronous or asynchronous interaction, both within a single address space or remotely.

An example for the second meaning (*interface inheritance*) is the programming language construct from the object-oriented language Java(tm):

```java
/* File name : Animal.java */
interface Animal {
    public void eat();
    public void move();
}


/* File name : Horse.java */
public class Horse implements Animal {
    public void eat() {
        System.out.println("Horse eats");
    }

    public void move() {
        System.out.println("Horse moves");
    }
}
```

Interface Segregation Principle (ISP)
Building blocks (classes, components) should not be forced to depend on methods they don't use.

ISP splits larger interfaces into smaller and more (client) specific ones so that clients will only need to know about methods that they actually use.

ISO9126

(Deprecated) standard to describe and evaluate *software product quality*. Has been superseded by → ISO 25010, see below.

ISO25010

Standards to describe (and evaluate) *software product quality*.

"The quality model determines which quality characteristics will be taken into account when evaluating the properties of a software product." (quote from the ISO website[45])

Iterative development

"Development approach that *cycles* through development phases, from gathering requirements to delivering functionality in a working release." (quoted from c2-wiki[46]). Such cycles are repeated to improve either functionality, quality or both.

Contrast with the → waterfall development.

Iterative and incremental development

Combination of iterative and incremental approaches for software development. These are essential parts of the various *Agile* development approaches, e.g. Scrum and Kanban. See LG 2-1 for a detailed explanation.

Latency

Latency is the time delay between the cause and the effect of some change in a system. In computer networks, latency describes the time it takes for an amount of data (*packet*) to get from one specific location to another. In interactive systems, latency is the time interval between some input to the system and the audio-visual response. Often a delay exists, frequently caused by network delays.

Layer

Grouping of building blocks or components that (together) offer a cohesive set of services to other layers.

Layers are related to each other by the ordered relation *allowed to use*.

Liskov substitution principle

Refers to object oriented programming: *If you use inheritance, do it right.*

Instances of derived types (subclasses) must be completely substitutable for their base types. If some code uses (*references*) a base class instance, these references can be replaced with any instance of a derived class without breaking that code.

—

45 http://iso25000.com/index.php/en/iso-25000-standards/iso-25010
46 http://c2.com/cgi/wiki?IterativeDevelopment

Microservice

An architectural style, proposing to divide large systems into small units.

"Microservices have to be implemented as virtual machines, as more light-weight alternatives such as Docker containers or as individual processes. Thereby they can easily be brought into production individually." (quoted from the free LeanPub booklet on Microservices[47] by Eberhard Wolff[48])

Model-Driven Architecture (MDA)

Model-Driven Architecture (MDA)[49] is an OMG-standard for model based software development.

Definition: "An approach to IT system specification that separates the specification of functionality from the specification of the implementation of that functionality on a specific technology platform."

Model-Driven Software Development (MDSD)

The underlying idea is to generate code from more abstract models of requirements or the domain.

Model-view controller

Architecture pattern, often used to implement user interfaces. It divides a system into three interconnected parts (model, view and controller) to separate the following responsibilities:

- Model manages data and logic of the system. The "truth" that will be shown or displayed by one or many views. Model does not know (depend on) its views.
- View can be any number of (arbitrary) output representations of (model) information. Multiple views of the same model are possible.
- Controller accepts (user) input and converts those to commands for the model or view.

Module

See also → modular programming.

1. Structural element or building block, usually regarded as a *black box* with a clearly defined responsibility. It encapsulates data and code and provides public interfaces, so clients can access its functionality. This meaning was first described in a groundbreaking and fundamental paper from David L. Parnas [Parnas1972].
2. In several programming languages, *module* is a construct for aggregating smaller programming units, e.g. in Python. In other languages (like Java), modules are called *packages*.

Modular programming

"Software design technique that separates the functionality of a program into independent, interchangeable *modules*, so that each module contains everything necessary to execute only one aspect of the desired functionality.

---

47 https://leanpub.com/microservices-primer
48 https://microservices-book.com
49 https://www.omg.org/mda/

Modules have *interfaces* expressing the elements provided and required by the module. The elements defined in the interface are detectable by other modules." (quoted from Wikipedia[50])

Node (in UML)

A processing resource (execution environment, processor, machine, virtual machine, application server) where artifacts can be deployed and executed.

Node (Node.js)

In modern web development: Short form for the open source JavaScript runtime Node.js[51], which is built on Chrome's V8 JavaScript engine.

Node.js is famous for its event-driven, non-blocking I/O model and its vast ecosystem of supporting libraries.

Non-functional requirement (NFR)

Requirements that *constrain the solution*.

Non-functional requirements are also known as *quality attribute requirements* or *quality requirements*.

The term NFR is actually misleading, as many of the *attributes* involved directly relate to specific system *functions* (so modern requirements engineering likes to call these things *required constraints*).

Notation

A system of marks, signs, figures or characters that is used to represent information. Examples include: prose, table, bullet point list, numbered list, UML, BPMN.

Observer

(Design pattern) "... in which an object, called the subject, maintains a list of its dependents, called observers, and notifies them automatically of any state changes, usually by calling one of their methods." (quoted from Wikipedia[52])

The Observer pattern is a key pattern to implement the → model–view–controller (MVC) architectural pattern.

Open-closed-principle (OCP)

"Software entities (classes, modules, functions, etc.) should be open for extension, but closed for modification" (Bertrand Meyer, 1998). In plain words:

To *add* functionality (extension) to a system, you should *not need to modify* existing code.

---

50 https://en.wikipedia.org/wiki/Modular_programming
51 https://nodejs.org/en/
52 https://en.wikipedia.org/wiki/Observer_pattern

Part of Robert Martin's "SOLID" principles for object-oriented systems. Can be implemented in object oriented languages by inheritance, in a more general way as *plugins.*

Pattern

A reusable or repeatable solution to a common problem in software design or architecture. See → architecture pattern or → design pattern.

Perspective

A perspective is used to consider a set of related quality properties and concerns of a system.

Architects apply perspectives iteratively to the system's *architectural views* in order to assess the effects of *architectural design decisions* across multiple *viewpoints* and *architectural views.*

[Rozanski+11] also associates the term *perspective* with activities, tactics and guidelines that must be considered if a system is to provide a set of related quality properties and suggests the following perspectives:
- Accessibility;
- Availability and resilience;
- Development resource;
- Evolution;
- Internationalization;
- Location;
- Performance and scalability;
- Regulation;
- Security;
- Usability.

Pipe

Connector in the pipes-and-filters architectural style that transfers streams or chunks of data from the output of one filter to the input of another filter without modifying values or order of data.

Port

UML construct, used in component diagrams. An interface, defining a point of interaction of a component with its environment.

POSA

Pattern-Oriented Software Architecture. Series of books on software architecture patterns.

Proxy

(Design pattern) "A wrapper or agent object that is being called by the client to access the real serving object behind the scenes. Use of the proxy can simply be forwarding to the real object, or can provide additional logic. In the proxy extra functionality can be provided, for example caching when operations on the real object are resource intensive, or checking preconditions before operations on the real object are invoked. For the client, usage of a proxy object is similar to using the real object, because both implement the same interface." (quoted from Wikipedia[53])

For details, see Part III on the proxy pattern.

Qualitative analysis

See → qualitative evaluation.

Qualitative evaluation

Finding risks concerning the desired quality attributes of a system.

Analyzing or assessing if a system or its architecture can meet the desired or required quality goals. Instead of calculating or measuring certain characteristics of systems or architectures, qualitative evaluation is concerned with risks, non-risks, trade-offs and sensitivity points.

 Personal opinion (Gernot): The term *evaluation* is misleading in this context, as it suggests that evaluation will result in *values* (metrics) - which is *not* the case! Instead this activity should better be named *qualitative analysis* or *software quality review*.

Quality

See → software quality and → quality attribute.

Quality attribute

Software quality is the degree to which a system possesses the desired combination of *attributes* (see: → software quality).

It's helpful to distinguish between:
- *Runtime quality attributes*, which can be observed at execution time of the system. Examples of runtime quality attributes are functional suitability, performance efficiency, security, reliability, availability, usability and interoperability.
- *Non-runtime quality attributes*, which cannot be observed as the system executes. Examples of non-runtime quality attributes are modifiability, portability, reusability, integrability, testability.
- *Business quality attributes*, like cost, schedule, marketability, appropriateness for organization.

See also → ISO 25010.

Quality characteristic

See → quality attribute.

---

53 https://en.wikipedia.org/wiki/Proxy_pattern

Quality model

(from ISO 25010) A model that defines quality characteristics that relate to static properties of software and dynamic properties of the computer system and software products.

The quality model provides consistent terminology for specifying, measuring and evaluating system and software product quality.

The scope of application of quality models includes supporting specification and evaluation of software and software-intensive computer systems from different perspectives by those associated with their acquisition, requirements, development, use, evaluation, support, maintenance, quality assurance and control, and audit.

Quality requirement

→ Quality attribute that a component of a system should exhibit or possess. Examples include runtime performance, safety, security, reliability or maintainability. See also → software quality.

Quality tree

(syn: quality attribute utility tree). A hierarchical model to describe product quality: The root "quality" is hierarchically refined in *areas* or topics, which itself are refined again. Quality scenarios form the leaves of this tree. Standards for product quality, like → ISO-25010, propose *generic* quality trees. The quality of a specific system can be described by a *specific* quality tree (see the example below).

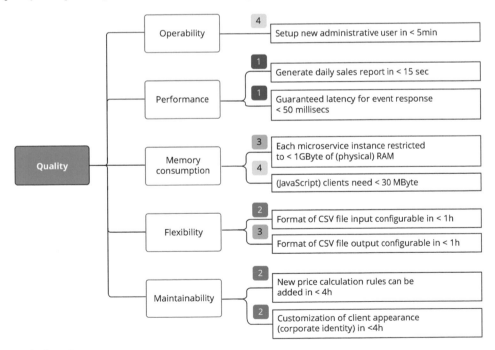

Example of a quality tree

The quality tree section in LG 4-2 contains a detailed explanation.

Quantitative analysis

See → quantitative evaluation.

Quantitative evaluation

(syn: quantitative analysis). Measure or count values of software artifacts, e.g. → coupling, → cyclomatic complexity, size, test coverage. Metrics like these can help to identify critical parts or elements of systems.

Rationale

Explanation of the reasoning or arguments that lie behind an architecture decision.

Redesign

The alteration of software units in such a way that they fulfill a similar purpose as before, but in a different manner and possibly by different means. Often mistakenly called refactoring.

Refactoring

A term denoting the improvement of software units by changing their internal structure without changing the behavior. (see "Refactoring is the process of changing a software system in such a way that it does not alter the external behavior of the code yet improves the internal structure." (Martin Fowler [Fowler+1999]). Not to be confused with → redesign.

Registry

"A well-known object that other objects can use to find common objects and services." (quoted from PoEAA[54]). Often implemented as a *Singleton* (also a well-known design pattern).

Relationship

Generic term denoting some kind of dependency between elements of an architecture. Different types of relationships are used within architectures, e.g. call, notification, ownership, containment, creation or inheritance.

Risk

Put simply, a risk is the possibility of a problem occurring. A risk involves *uncertainty* about the effects, consequences or implications of an activity or decision, usually with a negative connotation concerning a certain value (such as health, money, or qualities of a system like availability or security).

RM/ODP

The *Reference Model for Open Distributed Processing*[55] is an (abstract) metamodel for the documentation of information systems. Defined in ISO/IEC 10746.

---

54 https://martinfowler.com/eaaCatalog/registry.html
55 https://en.wikipedia.org/wiki/RM-ODP

Personal comment:
Not in broad use in Europe, and of very limited practical use for software development.

Round-trip engineering

"Concept of being able to make any kind of change to a model as well as to the code generated from that model. The changes always propagate bidirectionally and both artifacts are always consistent." (quoted from Wikipedia[56]).

Ruby

A wonderful programming language.

Runtime view

Shows the cooperation or collaboration between building blocks (respectively their instances) at runtime in concrete scenarios. Should refer to elements of the → building block view. Could for example (but doesn't need to) be expressed in UML sequence or activity diagrams.

Scenario

Quality scenarios document required quality attributes. They "... are brief narratives of expected or anticipated use of a system from both development and end-user viewpoints." [Kazman+1996]

Thus, they help to describe the required or desired qualities of a system in a pragmatic and informal manner, yet making the abstract notion of "quality" concrete and tangible. Usually scenarios are differentiated into:

- Usage scenarios (application scenarios);
- Change scenarios (modification or growth scenarios);
- Failure scenarios (boundary, stress, or exploratory scenarios).

For more details, see LG 4-2, on quality scenarios.

Self-contained system (SCS)

An architectural style, similar to → microservices.

To quote from the site scs-architecture.org:

"The self-contained system (SCS) approach is an architecture that focuses on a separation of the functionality into many independent systems, making the complete system a collaboration of many smaller software systems. This avoids the problem of large monoliths that grow constantly and eventually become unmaintainable."

Sensitivity point

(in qualitative evaluation like ATAM):

---

56 https://en.wikipedia.org/wiki/Model-driven_software_development

Element of the architecture or system influencing several quality attributes. For example, if one component is responsible for both runtime performance *and* robustness, that component is a sensitivity point. Casually said, if you mess up a sensitivity point, you will most often have more than one problem.

Separation of concerns (SoC)

Any element of an architecture should have exclusivity and singularity of responsibility and purpose: No element should share the responsibilities of another element or contain unrelated responsibilities. Another definition is "breaking down a system into elements that overlap as little as possible."

The famous Edgar Dijkstra said in 1974: "Separation of concerns ... even if not perfectly possible, is the only available technique for effective ordering of one's thoughts."

Similar to the → single responsibility principle.

Sequence diagram

Type of diagram to illustrate how elements of an architecture interact to achieve a certain scenario. It shows the sequence (flow) of messages between elements. As parallel vertical lines it shows the lifespan of objects or components. Horizontal lines depict interactions between these components. See the following example.

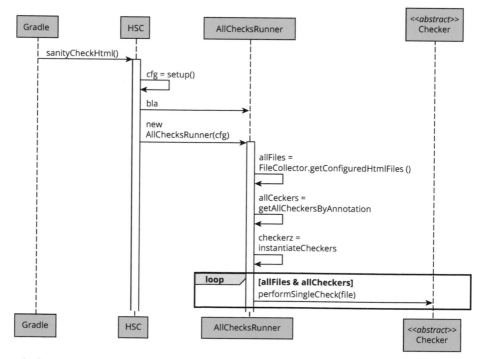

Example of a sequence diagram

Signature

Signature of function or method: See $\rightarrow$ function signature.

Digital signature: Method for verifying the authenticity of data or documents.

Singleton

"Design pattern that restricts the instantiation of a class to one object. This is useful when exactly one object is needed to coordinate actions across the system." (quoted from Wikipedia[57])

Single responsibility principle (SRP)

Each element within a system or architecture should have a single responsibility. All its functions or services should be aligned with that responsibility. $\rightarrow$ cohesion is sometimes considered to be associated with the SRP.

Software architecture

There exist several (!) valid and plausible definitions of the term *software architecture*. The following definition has been proposed by the IEEE 1471[58] standard:

> "Software architecture: the fundamental organization of a system embodied in its components, their relationships to each other and to the environment, and the principles guiding its design and evolution."

The new standard ISO/IEC/IEEE 42010:2011 has adopted and revised the definition as follows:

> "Architecture: (system) fundamental concepts or properties of a system in its environment embodied in its elements, relationships, and in the principles of its design and evolution."

The key terms in this definition require some explanation:
- **Components:** Subsystems, modules, classes, functions or the more general term *building blocks*. Structural elements of software. Components are usually implemented in a programming language, but can also be other artifacts that (together) *make up the system*.
- **Relationships:** Interfaces, dependencies, associations - different names for the same feature. Components need to interact with other components to enable *separation of concerns*.
- **Environment:** Every system has some relationships to its environment. Data, control flow or events are transferred to and from maybe different kinds of neighbors.
- **Principles:** Rules or conventions that hold for a system or several parts of it. Decision or definition, usually valid for several elements of the system. Often called *concepts* or even *solution patterns*. Principles (concepts) are the foundation for *conceptual integrity*.

The *Software Engineering Institute* maintains a collection of further definitions[59]

---

57   https://en.wikipedia.org/wiki/Singleton_pattern
58   https://en.wikipedia.org/wiki/IEEE_1471
59   https://www.sei.cmu.edu/architecture/start/glossary/classicdefs.cfm

Although the term often refers to the *software architecture of an IT system*, it is also used to refer to *software architecture as an engineering science*.

Software quality

(from IEEE Standard 1061): "Software quality is the degree to which software possesses a desired combination of attributes. This desired combination of attributes needs to be clearly defined; otherwise, assessment of quality is left to intuition."

(from ISO/IEC Standard 25010): "The quality of a system is the degree to which the system satisfies the stated and implied needs of its various stakeholders, and thus provides value. These stated and implied needs are represented in the ISO 25000 quality models that categorize product quality into characteristics, which in some cases are further subdivided into sub-characteristics."

S.O.L.I.D. principles

SOLID (single responsibility, open-closed, Liskov substitution, interface segregation and dependency inversion) is an acronym for some principles (named by Robert C. Martin) to improve object-oriented programming and design. The principles make it more likely that a developer will write code that is easy to maintain and extend over time.

Stakeholder

Person or organization that can be affected by, or have in interest (*stake*) in, a system, its development or execution.

Examples include users, employees, owners, administrators, developers, designers, product managers, product owners, project managers, requirements engineers, business-analysts, government agencies, enterprise architects etc.

Following ISO/IEC/IEEE 42010 a stakeholder is a (system) individual, team, organization, or classes thereof, having an interest in a system.

Such interest can be positive (e.g. stakeholder wants to benefit from the system), neutral (stakeholder has to test or verify the system) or negative (stakeholder is competing with the system or wants it to fail).

Structure

An arrangement, order or organization of interrelated elements in a system. Structures consist of building blocks (structural elements) and their relationships (dependencies).

Structures in software architecture are often used in → architectural views, e.g. the → building block view. A documentation template (e.g. → arc42) is a kind of structure too.

Structural element
See → building block or → component.

System
Collection of elements (building blocks, components, etc.) organized for a common purpose.

In ISO/IEC/IEEE standards a couple of system definitions are available:
- Systems as described in [ISO/IEC 15288]: "systems that are man-made and may be configured with one or more of the following: hardware, software, data, humans, processes (e.g., processes for providing service to users), procedures (e.g. operator instructions), facilities, materials and naturally occurring entities".
- Software products and services as described in [ISO/IEC 12207].
- Software-intensive systems as described in [IEEE Std 1471:2000]: "any system where software contributes essential influences to the design, construction, deployment, and evolution of the system as a whole" to encompass "individual applications, systems in the traditional sense, subsystems, systems of systems, product lines, product families, whole enterprises, and other aggregations of interest".

Template (for documentation)
Standardized order of artifacts used in software development. It can help to base other files, especially documents, in a predefined structure without prescribing the content of these single files. A well-known example of such templates is → arc42.

Temporal coupling
Different interpretations exist from various sources. Temporal coupling:
- Means that processes that are communicating will both have to be up and running. See [Tanenbaum+2016].
- When you often commit (*modify*) different components at the same time. See [Tornhill2015].
- When there's an implicit relationship between two, or more, members of a class requiring clients to invoke one member before the other. Mark Seemann, see
  https://blog.ploeh.dk/2011/05/24/DesignSmellTemporalCoupling/
- Means that one system needs to wait for the response of another system before it can continue processing.

TOGAF
TOGAF is a conceptual framework for the planning and maintenance of enterprise IT architectures. Not relevant for the iSAQB certification.

 Personal comment (Gernot)
No practical use for software development.

Personal comment (Alexander)

At least TOGAF somehow leads to the enterprise architecture modeling language ArchiMate[60] which is quite useful if you want to develop IT systems that support a large number of evolving business processes.

Top-down

"Direction of work" or "order of communication": Starting from an abstract or general construct working towards more concrete, special or detailed representation.

Traceability

(more precisely: *requirements* traceability): Document that:

- All requirements are addressed by elements of the system (forward traceability); and
- All elements of the system are justified by at least one requirement (backward traceability).

Personal comment

If you can, you should avoid or limit traceability, as it creates a lot of documentation overhead, which might never pay off.

However, in safety-critical systems, traceability is often a key requirement.

Trade-off

(syn: compromise). A balance achieved or negotiated between two desired or required features that are usually incompatible or contradicting.

For example, software development usually has to trade-off memory consumption and runtime performance.

More colloquially, if one thing increases, some other thing must decrease.

Even more colloquially: There is no free lunch. Every quality attribute has a price among other quality attributes.

Unified Modeling Language (UML)

UML (see http://uml.org) is a graphical language for visualizing, specifying and documenting the artifacts and structures of a software system. Some recommendations:

- For building block views or the context view, use component diagrams, with either components, packages or classes to denote building blocks.
- For runtime views, use sequence or activity diagrams (with swimlanes). Object diagrams can theoretically be used, but are practically not advised, as they become cluttered even for small scenarios.
- For deployment views, use deployment diagrams with node symbols.

---

60 https://en.wikipedia.org/wiki/ArchiMate

Unit test
Test of the smallest testable parts of system to determine whether they are fit for use.

Depending on implementation technology, a *unit* might be a method, function, interface or similar element.

Uses relation
Dependency that exists between two building blocks. If A uses B than execution of A depends on the presence of a correct implementation of B.

View
See → architectural view.

Waterfall development
Development approach "where you gather all the requirements up front, do all necessary design, down to a detailed level, then hand the specs to the coders, who write the code; then you do testing (possibly with a side trip to integration hell) and deliver the whole thing in one big end-all release. Everything is big including the risk of failure." (quoted from the C2 wiki[61])

Contrast to → iterative development.

White box
(often written *whitebox*)

Shows the internal structure of a system or building block, made up from black boxes and the internal/ external relationships and interfaces.

See also → black box.

Workflow management system (WFMS)
Provides an infrastructure for the set-up, performance and monitoring of a defined sequence of tasks, arranged as a workflow. (quoted from Wikipedia[62])

Wrapper
(syn: Decorator, Adapter) Patterns to abstract away the concrete interface or implementation of a component. Attach additional responsibilities to an object dynamically.

Depending on the sources, the semantics of the term *wrapper* may vary.

---

61 https://wiki.c2.com/?IterativeDevelopment
62 https://en.wikipedia.org/wiki/Workflow_management_system

Comment

The tiny differences found in literature regarding this term often don't matter in real-life. *Wrapping* a component or building block should have clear semantics within a single software system.

Appendix C: References and further reading

[arc42] arc42 - Template for Software Architecture Documentation. Open Source, published on https://arc42.org. A pragmatic, yet systematic structure for software architecture documentation, created by Peter Hruschka and Gernot Starke. In practical use since 2005, it has undergone various improvements. Excellent documentation (e.g. https://docs.arc42.org) plus numerous published examples. See also Communicating Software Architectures.

[Barbacci+2003] Mario Barbacci et al: Quality Attribute Workshops (QAWs), Third Edition. CMU/SEI-2003-TR-016. Software Engineering Institute, Carnegie Mellon University. 2003. http://resources.sei.cmu.edu/library/asset-view.cfm?AssetID=6687
This report describes one possible approach for deriving quality scenarios. Further background information can also be found in [Bass+2021].

[Bass+2021] Len Bass, Paul Clements, Rich Kazman: Software Architecture in Practice. Addison-Wesley; 4th edition, 2021.

[Brooks1975] Frederick P. Brooks: The mythical man-month: essays on software engineering. Addison-Wesley, 1975.

[Brown-C4]: Simon Brown: The C4 model for visualising software architecture. https://c4model.com. An introductory article on InfoQ: https://www.infoq.com/articles/C4-architecture-model.

[Brown2018] Simon Brown: Software Architecture For Developers, Leanpub, 2018. https://leanpub.com/software-architecture-for-developers
Very practical and pragmatic.

[Buschmann+1996] (aka: POSA-1) Frank Buschmann, Regine Meunier, Hans Rohnert, Peter Sommerlad, Michael Stal: Pattern Oriented Software Architecture, Volume 1: A System of Patterns, John Wiley & Sons, 1996.

[Buschmann+2007] (aka: POSA-4) Frank Buschmann, Kevlin Henneyand, Douglas Schmidt: Pattern-Oriented Software Architecture: A Pattern Language for Distributed Computing, 4th Volume, John Wiley & Sons, 2007.

[Cervantes+2016] Humberto Cervantes, Rick Kazman: Designing Software Architectures – A Practical Approach. SEI Series in Software Engineering, Pearson 2016.
Somewhat academic, proposes the ADD 3.0 Method (attribute-driven design).

[Clements+2002] Paul Clements, Rick Kazman, Mark Klein: Evaluating Software Architectures: Methods and Case Studies, Addison-Wesley, 2002. *Although quite dated, this is still the most extensive source for systematic qualitative analysis of software architectures. A concise and brief summary is given in [Bass+2021]*

[Clements+2010] Paul Clements, Felix Bachmann, Len Bass, David Garla et al: Documenting Software Architectures: Views and Beyond (SEI Series in Software Engineering) Addison- Wesley 2010.

[Cloud-Native] The Cloud Native Computing Foundation, online: https://www.cncf.io/

[DeMarco1995] Tom DeMarco: On Systems Architecture. in Proceedings of the 1995 Monterey Workshop Specification-Based Software Architectures, Calhoun, 1995. https://hdl.handle.net/10945/46121

[Evans2003] Eric Evans: Domain-Driven Design: Tackling Complexity in the Heart of Software. 1st edition, Addison-Wesley, 2003.
One of our all-time favorite books, although you need lots of patience to read through it. Some more recent textbooks provide simpler access to domain-driven design.

[Ford+17] Neil Ford, Rebecca Parsons, Patrick Kua: Building Evolutionary Architectures: Support Constant Change. OReilly 2017.

[Fowler2003] Martin Fowler: Patterns of Enterprise Application Architecture. Addison-Wesley, 2002. *Great support for building information systems, one of our favorites.*

[Gamma+1995] Erich Gamma, Richard Helm, Ralph Johnson, John Vlissides: Design Patterns: Elements of Reusable Object-Oriented Software. Addison-Wesley, 1994.
A classic.

[Geewax-2020] J.J. Geewax: API Design Patterns. Manning Publications 2020. *The authors was responsible for the design of several public APIs at Google, especially in the cloud infrastructure.*

[Hargis+2004] Gretchen Hargis, Michelle Carey, Ann Hernandez: Developing Quality Technical Information: A Handbook for Writers and Editors. IBM Press, 2nd edition, Prentice Hall, 2004. *If you need to write lots of documentation, you should have a look at this book.*

[Hofmeister+1999] Christine Hofmeister, Robert Nord, Dilip Soni: Applied Software Architecture, a Practical Approach. 1st edition, Addison-Wesley, 1999.
The authors present the global analysis method to systematically achieve quality requirements and analyze their mutual trade-offs or dependencies.

[Hohpe+2003] Gregor Hohpe, Bobby Woolf: Enterprise Integration Patterns: Designing, Building, and Deploying Messaging Solutions. Addison Wesley, 2003.
In Gernot's opinion, one of the most important books for people creating integrated systems.

[IREB]: International Requirements Engineering Board: Handbook Advanced Module "RE@Agile", https://www.ireb.org/de/downloads/tag:advanced-level-re-agile

[iSAQB-FLC] iSAQB-Foundation Level Curriculum, https://public.isaqb.org/curriculum-foundation/

[ISO-12207] ISO/IEC/IEEE 12207:2017 Systems and software engineering — Software lifecycle processes, 2017. https://www.iso.org/standard/63712.html
Provides a process framework for describing the lifecycle of systems.

[ISO-25010] ISO/IEC 25010:2011 Systems and software engineering - Systems and software Quality Requirements and Evaluation (SQuaRE) - System and software quality models, 2010. https://www.iso.org/standard/35733.html
Defines a generic model for software (product) quality.

[Kazman+2000] Rick Kazman, Mark Klein, Paul Clements: ATAM: Method for Architecture. CMU/SEI-2000-TR-004. Software Engineering Institute, Carnegie Mellon University. 2000. https://resources.sei.cmu.edu/library/asset-view.cfm?AssetID=5177

[Keeling2017] Michael Keeling: Design It!, From Programmer to Software Architect. The Pragmatic Programmer LLC, 2017.
A very pragmatic book that follows ideas and concepts quite close to stuff given in the iSAQB Foundation Curriculum, although sometimes with a very different terminology.

[Kruchten-1995] Philippe Kruchten: *The 4+1 View Model of Architecture*, IEEE Software, volume 12 (6), pp 45-50, 1995. Available online: https://bit.ly/3gR9ACt

[Larman+2003] Craig Larman, Victor Basil: Iterative and Incremental Development: A Brief History, Computer 36.6, 2003. Available online: https://www.craiglarman.com/wiki/downloads/misc/history-of-iterative-larman-and-basili-ieee-computer.pdf

[Martraire2019] Martraire, Cyrille: Living Documentation - *Continous Knowledge Sharing By Design*. Addison-Wesley, 2019.

[Newman2015] Sam Newman: Building Microservices: Designing Fine-Grained Systems. O'Reilly. 2015.

[North-BDD] Dan North: *Introducing Behavior-Driven Development.*
https://dannorth.net/introducing-bdd/

[Nygard2018] Michael T. Nygard: Release It! Design and Deploy Production-Ready Software.
Pragmatic Bookshelf; 2nd edition, 2018.

[Nygard2022] Michael Nygard: CUPID - for joyful coding. See https://dannorth.net/2022/02/10/cupid-for-joyful-coding/ .

[Nygard-ADR] Michael Nygard: Documenting Architecture Decision.
https://cognitect.com/blog/2011/11/15/documenting-architecture-decisions.
See also https://adr.github.io/

[Parnas1972] David Parnas: On the criteria to be used in decomposing systems into modules.
Communications of the ACM, volume 15, issue 12, Dec 1972.
Possibly one of the most influential articles ever written in software engineering.

[Pierce2002] Benjamin C. Pierce: Types and Programming Languages. MIT Press. 2002.

[Quian+2010] Kai Qian, Xiang Fu, Lixin Tao, Chong-Wei Xu, Jorge L. Díaz-Herrera: Software
Architecture and Design Illuminated. 1st edition, Jones and Bartlett, 2010.
Well-structured and readable collection of architecture styles and patterns.

[Q42] arc42 Quality Model, online: https://quality.arc42.org

[Rajlich+2000] Václav T. Rajlich, Keith H. Bennett: A staged model for the software lifecycle. Computer
33.7 (2000).

[Req4Arc] Requirements for Architects (Req4Arc) Advanced Level Module Curriculum:
https://isaqb-org.github.io/curriculum-req4arc/

[Richards-2015]: Mark Richards: Software Architecture Patterns:
https://learning.oreilly.com/library/view/software-architecture-patterns/9781491971437/

[Richardson-2018] Chris Richardson: Microservice Patterns, Manning 2018. Several patterns accessible online: https://microservices.io/patterns/microservices.html

[Rozanski+11] Nick Rozanski, Eoin Woods: Software Systems Architecture - Working with
Stakeholders Using Viewpoints and Perspectives. 2nd Edition, Addison Wesley 2011.
Presents a set of architectural viewpoints and perspectives.

[Schmidt+2000] Douglas Schmidt, Michael Stal, Hans Rohnert, Frank Buschmann: Pattern-Oriented Software Architecture, volume 2: Patterns for Concurrent and Networked Objects. 1st edition, Wiley & Sons, 2000.

[Shaw+1996] Mary Shaw, David Garlan: Software Architecture: Perspectives on an Emerging Discipline, Prentice Hall, 1996.

[Starke+2019] G. Starke, R. Müller, M. Simons, S. Zörner: arc42 by Example. Software Architecture Documentation in Practice. Packt Publishing, 2019.

Also available as Leanpub eBook Online: https://leanpub.com/arc42byexample/
Six real-world systems documented and explained with the arc42 template. Contentwise the print version and the Leanpub version are (nearly) identical.

[Starke+2016] Gernot Starke, Peter Hruschka: Communicating Software Architectures: lean, effective and painless documentation. Leanpub: https://leanpub.com/arc42inpractice

[Tanenbaum+2016] Andrew Tanenbaum, Maarten van Steen: Distributed Systems, Principles and Paradigms. https://www.distributed-systems.net/

[Tornhill2015] Adam Tornhill: Your Code as a Crime Scene. Use Forensic Techniques to Arrest Defects, Bottlenecks, and Bad Design in Your Programs. Pragmatic Programmers, 2015. https://www.adamtornhill.com

[UML] Universal Modeling Language, homepage: http://uml.org/. Provides both the standard plus a collection of resources for further information.

See also:
- A pragmatic collection of information concerning UML diagrams: https://www.uml-diagrams.org/

[Yorgey] Brent Yorgey: Monoids - Theme and Variations. Proceedings of the 2012 Haskell Symposium, September 2012 Pages 105–116, https://doi.org/10.1145/2364506.2364520

[Zimmermann+2015] O. Zimmermann, L. Wegmann, H. Koziolek, T. Goldschmidt: Architectural Decision Guidance Across Projects - Problem Space Modeling, Decision Backlog Management and Cloud Computing Knowledge, 12th Working IEEE/IFIP Conference on Software Architecture, Montreal, QC, 2015.

Index